SURVIVE, THEN THRIVE

Understanding Post-Traumatic Stress

PRAISE FOR *"SURVIVE, THEN THRIVE"*

A compelling and poignant memoir. Onlock's heart-centred exploration of her journey with PTSD is raw and real, encouraging the reader to confront their own biases and inner demons (and come out the other side better for having done so). This a must-read, not only for anyone who suffers with PTSD and those with loved ones who have experienced PTSD, but also for everyone who has faced adversity themselves and/or with a loved one. This important book will inspire understanding and healing and is a game-changer on the issue.

Cindy Watson, award-winning and best-selling author of *The Art of Feminine Negotiation* and *Out of Darkness*.

SURVIVE, THEN THRIVE

Understanding Post-Traumatic Stress

Peggy Onlock

ISBN: 978-1-962825-18-4

Atlas Elite Publishing Partners

ATLAS ELITE
PUBLISHING
PARTNERS

Women on Purpose Publishing

WOMEN on
PURP♀SE

This book is a labour of love and a new found strength dedicated to all who have been impacted by crime and/or tragic circumstances and have suffered the recurring pain of Post-Traumatic Stress symptoms as a result of those experiences. Know that you have an amazing strength despite the self-doubt and confusion your past experiences cause within you. Search out the supports and positive influences around you. You can process the traumas that you experienced in the past and move forward with a newfound peace and understanding.

And to my parents, David and Barbara;

My brothers, Dave, Rick and Robert

My sister, Kathryn

And my nieces and nephew, Elizabeth, Rachel and Paul

Your presence, even when it was from a distance gave me a strength and desire to work through these most difficult parts of my life and put pen to paper

CONTENTS

INTRODUCTION

I NEVER REALLY BELIEVED THAT WHEN YOU DIE, YOUR LIFE FLASHES before you. A series of images from your past, each a glimpse into what led you to this moment. The good moments, like coffee with new friends; the momentous life occasions, like the birth of a child or graduation; and the bad, like losing your parent, or hard life lessons that intermingle with a swiftness that makes them blur into a single image: yourself. And now that you've come face to face with it, what do you do? How do you react?

No, I'd never really believed that when you die, your life flashes before you. That is, until I experienced what I now know as symptoms of PTSD. I've often thought of it and explained it like my relational database was out of whack. Absolutely everything reminded me of some time, somebody, or something that I had experienced during my lifetime. And because of the extreme stress I was feeling at the time, I thought the vivid memories or flashbacks that I re-experienced would be the death of me … literally. The folders of my mind that normally compartmentalize ideas and information to make sense of them were thrown into the air and blended. Events that reminded me of others triggered a memory and got mixed up, especially in sequencing my history.

Life takes us many places that we do not choose and would prefer never to visit. My most important breakthrough came when I acknowledged these were just places to visit and didn't have to be permanent destinations. It is possible to break the cycles that take you to a persistent and unforgiving past. It is also possible to finally include the part of your story that once brought you to your knees, without the dramatic and sometimes deadly symptoms of Post-Traumatic Stress Disorder (PTSD).

For years I dreamed of putting pen to paper and let years of experience be heard and make some sense of it all; not only by others but by myself. Sometimes to see things more clearly, you must make sense of the confusion and absurdity of life itself. Silent words and thoughts were so loud they were almost deafening. They screamed to come out but I couldn't seem to let them flow out of my mouth so I could finally be free of them.

I am glad that I can tell this story now, in what I hope is a safe place to increase the awareness that we need when it comes to facing mental health challenges in a way that will encourage recovery and support.

This story is from my perspective, so I know it will not speak to everyone. I'm an introvert who cherishes her privacy and would prefer to let the extroverts of the world be the ones with the loudest voices. But not always as the introvert often has a deep understanding of life itself, especially after decades of looking analytically at one's own life of turmoil and resilience. The introversion that allowed me to analyse myself is what gives me the perspective to tell my own story as only I can tell it.

There will be some uncomfortable conversations, but some clarifying and uplifting ones as well. Leaving out significant events doesn't change the fact that they happened, or make the impacts go away. Their avoidance only allows them to forever fester and leave huge gaps that prevent you from processing your narrative. I have not written anything too graphic, but also haven't left out significant events simply because they are horrible. I left out some names to protect the privacy of those impacted and avoid the tarring and feathering of the bystanders for a time when they chose the only way they knew to handle those frightening events.

You will see several themes throughout this book portraying significant patterns throughout life. I hope this exercise illustrates how and why PTSD symptoms that cause the resurgence of memories can be so disturbing and sometimes deadly.

And I hope this book will help people understand what a person with PTSD can experience and the impact of those experiences. I hope it will clarify some misconceptions about PTSD. Most of all, I hope it will bring awareness and inner peace to someone.

But first, it's important to have context. Our history, our past, and our experiences affect and connect us, and post-traumatic stress illustrates those impacts and connections in detail.

Here is my story.

PART ONE

CHAPTER ONE

━━━━◆━━━━

Setting the Scene, Background History

I T STARTS MORE THAN FIFTY YEARS AGO IN A CITY THAT HAD become home to a large extended family. In my early years, I had close relationships with my immediate family. I was fortunate enough to have a close relationship with some of my extended family too, who also played a big part in my younger years. For example, my paternal grandparents babysat us when we were younger as both of my parents worked.

I was especially close to my aunt, Ida, who I could go to for support or when I needed someone to lean on. She understood me better than most, as she had been through some similar experiences when she was young. Our similar experiences created a strong bond between us.

My family history was always important to me, even as a child. My parents are Canadian. My maternal grandfather was from a well-to-do Newfoundland family, and my maternal grandmother was from the mining town of Stellarton, Nova Scotia. They married when my grandmother was only 16 years old. My grandfather was disowned shortly after because his family didn't approve of the marriage.

My maternal grandparents eventually found their way to Toronto, Ontario after several stops and several children throughout Canada (and even one in the state of Massachusetts). My mother was born in Toronto, the youngest of twelve children: six girls and six boys.

My paternal grandfather came to Canada from Romania as a teenager in 1914, amidst the chaos of World War 1. We never knew if he came here alone or not, nor did we ever know his real last name or family history. All he left us about his history was one small brochure with limited information, including his parents' names, Michael and Anna, and that he was raised in an Eastern Orthodox family before making his journey to Canada. When he arrived, he was placed in an internment camp in Kapuskasing, Ontario, both because he didn't have any papers and because he was from Eastern Europe. One possibility my family considered was that my grandfather was born Jewish and raised by an Eastern Orthodox family, leaving his homeland to escape the harsh treatment of Eastern European Jews. I'll never know if this is the truth, but it's a possibility that will form the memories of my grandfather until the day that I die.

My paternal grandmother was from a small town in Near North, Ontario. She was of Irish descent and proud of it. Her story, too, was somewhat tragic. History indicates her father came to Canada as a child from Carrickmacross,

County Monaghan, Ireland during the potato famine. His parents were tenant farmers in Ireland, not too far from the border of what is now Northern Ireland and the Republic of Ireland. They died on the way to Canada. My great grandfather was taken in by a family who settled in Near North, Ontario. The saddest part of that story, to me, is that they were made to change the spelling of their name so they were no longer seen as Irish Catholic.

My grandmother lived in a log cabin until she married and found her way to the Sudbury area and then Southern Ontario. My father was born in that log cabin. He was one of six children: 3 girls and 3 boys. As the second oldest and eldest male child, he worked from the age of 13 to help feed his family. His father had been a builder but lost the ability to do that job due to injury.

Near North is still probably the place where I feel the strongest connection to my history. The place where I could see the beginnings of my family. A place to call home. Toronto is my real hometown and I love it dearly. But it has never had the same effect on me as northern Ontario where I am immediately taken back in time to the roots of my family's new beginning in Canada.

I think of my grandmother as a little girl tending the animals that were kept for milk, eggs, and food for the family. Apparently, she always made pets of the farm animals, just like I would have, and couldn't bring herself to eat any of the chickens or other animals that had been raised on her family's plot of land.

I think of the stories I heard from my older family members of the hardships they endured living in a small log cabin just outside of town.

The cabin had been relocated onto the property of a more distant relative by the time I saw it. When I was young it looked like it was in pretty good shape but when I went to visit in middle age, it was dilapidated and unsafe to enter. I remember peeking in the window and the floor was unsafe to walk on. Somebody had placed a star over the front door. I doubt if that had been there when my grandmother and father lived there years before.

The star and the fact that the cabin had been moved created uneasy questions in my mind and didn't seem authentic. When I was younger and even to this day, it seemed to be super imposed on a previous and more authentic history.

Still, the forests around it, the parkland and river all brought peace to me and memories of my father's and grandparent's childhoods. They would have been harsh, but there was love in the family and they truly cared for each other. My paternal grandparents also met around that area, and it would have been the start of my immediate family.

Since the cabin wasn't in its original location, I always dreamed of moving it to another place so my family could visit a pleasant part of our roots.

My paternal grandparents moved to Toronto with 6 young children. By that time my maternal grandparents were already in Toronto.

I think the farm was my dad's first home in the city, before it became part of what is now a sprawling city. My grandfather was a builder so was well able to make a home for his family. They rented the farmhouse to my mom's family members.

That would be where mom and dad met in their teens. I remember my mother telling me she knew as early as 13 years old that she would marry my dad.

They did marry as soon as my mom was of legal age. They had a good marriage and it was obvious there was much love in their relationship. They extended that love to their family and ensured we were able to have strong relationships within our extended families as well.

We didn't always get to spend a lot of time together as we aged because distance would keep us apart physically. But the bond was always there, and still is.

Mom often told me her parents weren't thrilled when she married young, but both sets of grandparents came to appreciate this union and their choice of spouses.

I was fortunate to know both sets of grandparents, as my mom and dad opened our house to them as I was growing up. I often think of how wonderful it was that I knew both sets of grandparents into my teens.

FINDING WORK IN A NEW PROVINCE

When I was a year old, my parents decided to go to Alberta. My father didn't find work there and they were far away from family. They soon decided to move back to Ontario to find work closer to home and be closer to our extended family. My father became a police officer. My mother had worked at the bank since she was 15 years old.

Mom started working at a bank in her community because her father was unable to pay back a bank loan. He spoke to the bank manager who agreed my mother could work there to repay the loan. I thought of that as child labour, and a horrible thing to do to your daughter.

Mom worked at banks for many years and was good at her job and very well-respected among her peers. I later worked at the same bank and got to know many of the same people. I appreciated that they always told me what a nice person my mother was. I knew that firsthand.

CHAPTER TWO

Childhood Abuse and Some Impacts

WHEN I WAS NEARLY 5 YEARS OLD, MY PARENTS, MY TWO OLDER brothers, and I moved to a small town about an hour from Toronto, Ontario. My early years included many moves. Even with the constant upheaval and financial insecurity due to our rapidly growing family, the love of our family ensured this didn't throw anyone into despair. We always knew things would work out, and they did.

I had a happy childhood. I got along well with my siblings and we did a lot of things together. We played, went camping, and rode bikes. The bikes were an issue every now and then because I always wanted to ride my brother's bike before I had my own. I got banged up a few times along the way, but always had two older brothers to help me through the pain.

When I was quite young, my paternal grandparents lived with us and looked after us while my parents worked. Dad was on shift work, so we had to adjust our schedules so he could get some sleep when he was on midnights. I also remember adjusting our Christmas plans to coincide with his shift, but we always enjoyed family time together.

I loved our family camping vacations, usually to eastern Canada and the US, but sometimes into the Great Lakes region of the Northern US and Canada. They were great vacations.

Then, one summer, my parents agreed to take in the young student pastor of our church. He was from Montreal and had been adopted or was being cared for by someone fairly high up in the church hierarchy. He went to the seminary in Toronto and had been placed in our small church out of town so needed a place to live for the summer. We had an extra room so my parents agreed he could live with us for the summer.

While he lived with us, he took me under his wing and began teaching me Bible verses. We spent a lot of time together while my parents were at work. Nobody knew until several years later that as he was teaching me Bible verses, he was also molesting me. This continued for several years as he came back for other work opportunities in our church. Though he only stayed with my family for one summer, he would continue to 'teach me' in the church study after we moved when he had the opportunity.

He only lived with us that one summer. When he returned the following year, he was able to move in with another family. I don't remember how I felt other than glad he wasn't living with us. I still would have been very young and didn't comprehend what had happened.

I finally reported the dirty secret of childhood molestation when I got into a rare argument with one of my brothers. Arguing with my brothers was not a normal occurrence as we usually got along quite well. We were reprimanded by my parents for our argument and behaviour. In a hysterical fit, I shouted out that if they didn't have a bunch of pigs living with us none of it would ever have happened. Hysterics were very out of character for me. I only remember one other time as a child when I went into hysterics, and that was when I witnessed my beloved dog, Toby, get killed by a truck in front of our house. I was off school for a week. But this outburst was different. As I mentioned before, my father was a police officer. This might have been part of the reason why he knew something was terribly wrong. He asked me what I was talking about, as my reaction seemed to him to be the result of some deeper issue and not a simple matter of sibling disagreement. I finally told him I had been molested.

I remember parts of the aftermath of that disclosure quite vividly. Our world was turned upside down. Police were called in to investigate. They questioned me in the basement of the church. My parents were with me. At one point the police asked me to go sit further away from the adults so they could speak to my parents privately. This bothered me. I could hear them talking about me as if I wasn't there. But I *was* there and it was *me* they were talking about.

I don't recall hearing my parents discussing the case at home, but I was certainly impacted because I felt I was the cause of our moving yet again to another community. I felt I was the one who tore my siblings away from their friends, their schools, and their community.

I realized that my family was, for the most part, alone. This impacted me deeply and it was only the beginning. I felt guilty for reporting the crime and guilty for not reporting it sooner. It was an extremely confusing time for me and had a huge impact on me over the years. I felt alone and that my family had been betrayed by the church members and especially, the young pastor and his family.

I was being run out of town with my family because I had been assaulted and reported it; even though that reporting was quite by accident and I certainly didn't understand the severity of the crimes at that time.

The perpetrator pled guilty and was given 6 months psychiatric treatment. I don't recall hearing a lot about it at the time and the case was kept very hush-hush; I think, more to protect my identity at the time. In the 1960's and 1970's there was much victim-blaming, and sexual crimes were often considered the fault of the victim regardless of their age. They still are, but we are gaining awareness in that area of criminal justice.

In addition to that, the reputation of a religious organization was at risk of being damaged. I vaguely recalled that the perpetrator had received a light sentence to rehabilitate him but didn't understand it at the time. In fact, for years, I had forgotten about it altogether. When the perpetrator showed up at our doorstep decades later to apologize, I asked my father what had happened with the court case. I'll discuss this in a later chapter.

Much of what I know about the community reaction is from later discussions with people I've remained in contact with over the years. It helped me piece together and explain some of my feelings over the years as well.

PART TWO

MID – JOURNEY. ALONG THE WAY

CHAPTER THREE

Teenage Angst

DRUGS

∞

NOT LONG AFTER, MY FAMILY MOVED TO ANOTHER SMALL TOWN. It wasn't that far away but was in another policing jurisdiction and would mean new schools and a new church for our family. We maintained a few friendships from our earlier years, including one girl I remain friends with to this day, but for the most part we started a new life. This was a good thing at the time, at least for me. A new start, but still within a comfortable drive to visit family in Toronto. It was a nice enough town, but I quickly found out that it wasn't far enough away from the gossip. Growing up with that knowledge in my community was hard.

During my teen years, I felt inferior because of my past. I felt damaged, like people were looking down on me and talking behind my back. People who knew about my past judged me, and for some reason they felt it was alright to let me know their thoughts about it. When I was 14 or 15 years old, my friend and I were sitting at the fairground with my two cousins, both named John. My friend's mother came into the tower, screaming, "Do you know what this looks like?!" and that we shouldn't be there. All she could see was two girls and two boys without supervision, and my past made her connect the dots into something preposterous.

The judgement from my community had a serious impact on me and I soon found myself with few friends except for the 'troubled' kids. My first experience with drugs was when someone dropped LSD into my drink. I was probably around 13 years old. I remember the terror of the hallucinations and crouching in the bathroom while someone tried to talk me down from a really bad trip. I think I tried it once or twice after that just because the other kids were, and I also wanted to convince myself it couldn't have been that bad. I was wrong. This was not the end of my bad experiences with drugs. I had an older cousin involved with someone who used speed, and they convinced me to try it once. I remember it being injected into my arm, but nothing after that. I never did it again.

By that time, many people considered me a drug addict, but I don't think I was an addict. I would go for very long periods of time without any substance use at all. Truth be told, I tried a few illegal drugs, including marijuana, LSD, and speed. But my drug use was usually 222's that I took for headaches, diet pills because I thought I was too fat, or alcohol. I didn't purchase drugs, except a few tablets of LSD and a few joints. The kids and young adults who were in the drug culture were always willing to share and didn't want to experience the high alone.

I was stupid and rebellious enough at that age to allow people, including my family, to believe my drug use was worse than it was. I would sometimes even puncture the crook in my elbow to make it look like needle marks. I hadn't injected anything but went along with the rumours of the day. That being said, any drugs can be deadly, so it was something that had to stop. It also didn't provide the escape that I wanted and needed at that time; especially the LSD that created horrible and terrifying images for me. I quit when I was 15 but didn't let on that I was now clean. This was mainly because I thought if I did, I would be stuck in time, stuck in a small town where nothing would change.

Before we moved back to the city, my father reached out to a health professional from my previous town where the initial assault had occurred. They arranged for me to attend a short program at the Addiction Research Foundation (ARF) in Toronto. It was an in-house counselling program for people with drug and alcohol issues. My family was moving back to Toronto by this time, but I went back ahead of them to attend this inpatient counselling program. It was good because it dealt with the issues that I was having with the earlier childhood assault and my very low self-esteem. The counsellors were excellent. I remember one in particular, who was a young draft dodger from the US who decided against fighting in the Vietnam War.

Even at that young age, I thought leaving your country and family had to be difficult and was an honourable thing to do if for good reason. It was also honourable not to fight when you didn't believe in fighting a war that was not just. I was still in my mid-teens, but old enough to see the Vietnam War in the news often and form an opinion. I was close enough to the US to know others who had come to Canada to avoid the draft and violence. To me, that was courageous. I knew enough about war at the time to know that it's a very serious decision and should be the last resort any country should take to resolve conflict. It was something I felt (and still feel) is wrong when it's to exert power and injustices against a country for your own benefit or expansion. I also felt (and still feel) that serving your country is one of the highest honours. But conscription wasn't something I support. I believe people have to make that choice for themselves.

This often reminded me of my mother's older brother, who died in WWII and is buried in the Netherlands. My grandmother reminisced about him, telling me he was the son who least wanted to fight. He joined the military out of a sense of duty to his country. His two brothers had joined with the excitement of impending battles and seeing the world. I often thought my uncle who didn't return must have been a peaceful man, and his life was cut too short in a war that he didn't particularly want to fight. That's what war was to me, whether it be WWII or the Vietnam War, where our choice to live was at risk of being taken away by someone else. I always thought our own living or dying was the ultimate decision that we should be able to control as much as possible, not be imposed on us by another human being, or government.

The counsellor at ARF and I talked mostly about me, of course. The thing I most remember was that he treated me like I was my own person and deserving of respect. He was probably in his twenties or thirties, although at the young age of 15, I still considered anyone over 21 as old. He was a calm, caring person who reminded me over and over that the childhood assault was not my fault and I had done nothing to deserve it. I recall him telling me that drug abuse was often a result of assault and the inability to cope with the trauma. He was also very specific in telling me that the past was the past and I was able to move forward and lead a better life where my past traumas didn't have to impact me as much. Of course, there was also the drug abuse. He reiterated that was not a solution and would only create many more serious issues. He was right.

When I completed the program, I went to live with my Aunt Ida and her husband in Toronto. My parents were moving back to Toronto a few months later. I joined them when they did. My parents felt it would be best if I lived with my aunt and uncle for a short time rather than moving back to the town where I was having so many issues. I supported that decision fully but was glad when my parents moved back to the city and I could rejoin the rest of my immediate family. I still lived close enough to my aunt and uncle that we spent a lot of time together.

My mother wasn't comfortable speaking to me about personal female things in my younger years (unless it was an argument during my years of teenage rebellion). Mom also thrived on an argument, or what she called "a debate". She usually sent me to speak to my aunt when I was feeling bad or starting a new phase in my life. When I started menstruating in Grade 7 and thought I was bleeding to death because of my ignorance, I ran to my aunt who explained it to me. We also shared a trauma bond since she had personal experience dealing with some of the issues I was having. She had been molested as a child by a step-cousin. Throughout her teenage years, she had two children out of wedlock and an addiction to alcohol. I felt that her past mirrored my present, so I felt more comfortable with her than I did with my own mother. My aunt was a godsend to me in that most difficult period of my life.

HIGH SCHOOL

∞

High school, of course, brought its own set of challenges. I befriended a girl, Jane, who happened to know much of my sordid past thanks to neighbourhood gossip. One of the first conversations we had was when she told me she knew what happened to me when I was younger. Her mother had been told by a lady from the small town we had lived in, and she told her daughter. Jane, immediately made it her business. What Jane didn't know she was more than willing to exaggerate to make more dramatic. In some cases, she completely fabricated the truth if it didn't meet her expectations of intrigue and drama. I often thought she was living vicariously through me to impose her feelings of superiority over me. At the time, I didn't realize how badly Jane's "friendship" was affecting me; I think I was just grateful to have a friend. Or at least to have the illusion of friendship, because she did nothing to comfort me in my times of need like a real friend should.

I remember on one occasion walking down the hall at school with my wrist bandaged. The art teacher stopped and laughingly asked, "Did you try to kill yourself?" I hadn't but am sure I felt it wouldn't have been much of a loss if I did. I don't recall talking about it a lot, but was feeling badly that my friends, including Jane, didn't show any compassion and found it funny. They did little, if anything, to comfort me. I recall leaving art class soon afterwards because I felt uncomfortable in a room with that teacher.

Another time, after having left that school, I went back for a dance. By that time, I'd found a full-time job in Toronto that I was quite proud of. I mentioned it to the guidance counsellor who was chaperoning the event. While at school, I don't recall many interactions with her at all. I mentioned my new job to the guidance counsellor, probably to let her know that I had overcome my issues and turned my life around. I'm sure she would have been aware of my issues because I left school and there was a lot of gossip among students and teachers in the school. She responded in a very condescending tone of voice, that she always thought I would end up on the streets. This attitude was common among a few teachers and fellow students in school. I felt worthless and doomed to their predictions at the time. In all fairness, I do recall my history teachers and vice principal being very supportive and treating me well.

The guidance counsellor's response upset me. I was proud I'd turned my young life around and felt she really insulted me by insinuating it was a fluke. I wondered why on earth she thought it was appropriate to respond in that way. I still wonder that at times, though her opinion of me doesn't impact me like it did when I was in my teens.

I recall talking to Jane about this, and as usual, she thought it was funny. My response, as usual, was to keep it all in and go on as if nothing had happened. I felt like I was the weak one for not being to cope with the insults.

I eventually quit high school because I couldn't stand it anymore. I figured I was doomed from the start because of my past. The stigma had already attached to me as a "damaged" kid, and I didn't get much encouragement from teachers or students during most of my high school education. There were a few exceptions. The vice principal was always kind and helped me throughout the years. My grade 10 history teacher always treated me with respect, like a human being with potential. He even came to visit me at the ARF when I was going through counselling. But even this support was not enough to make me comfortable staying in school around the faculty who judged me and the peers who bullied me. I left after completing Grade 10.

LEAVING HIGH SCHOOL BEHIND

∞

When I left school after Grade 10, it was around the time my family moved back to Toronto. I was transitioning from the move from my aunt's home to my family home again, so I had a choice of high schools. I tried attending Grade 11 in Toronto but left part way through the academic year because I found it too difficult to cope. I felt the teachers and students at the new school treated me much better but there were just too many reminders. The only things I remember from the new school are learning to be a tree in drama class, and my red-haired history teacher. I think I remembered the tree because it let me learn something creative without even opening my mouth. I remember this history teacher, partly because I loved history and he, like those before him, treated me kindly and with respect.

I kept in touch with some of my friends after moving back to the city, but for the most part fell out of touch with them. Jane and I kept in touch periodically, but I didn't really feel like she was a close friend. Our paths crossed again when she moved to Toronto to attend university, and again, when my mother helped her get a job at the bank.

My parents were supportive because they wanted what was best for me and my mental health at that time. They knew how difficult it was for me and supported my decision to leave school and find a job.

I don't have a lot of recollections about what happened right after leaving high school again, but I did find a job quickly. I believe that was the job that I mentioned to the guidance counsellor in the previous chapter. I liked that job but felt I had really missed out on my education. I decided to go back to school and looked into my options. When I think about it now, I'm quite impressed that my high school experience didn't completely destroy my desire to learn. There were enough good experiences to balance the bad, so I left that option as a possibility in the future.

I found a college course that would allow me to achieve my Grade 13 equivalency and attend either college or university afterwards.

In the first years after returning to Toronto, several of my friends were able to come and board with us for a period of time while they searched for jobs in the city. I still remain in touch with several of them to this day.

CHAPTER FOUR

Rejoining the World Through Work and School

AS MENTIONED, ONE OF THE THINGS THAT ALWAYS BOTHERED ME, even in my late teens, was that I never graduated from high school. I felt I had missed out learning about things that really interested me; especially subjects like history and geography. I was also aware that it would be difficult to find a better job with only Grade 10 by that time. College, here I come!

My time at college was interesting, to say the least. It was not like high school. I took regular high school courses, like math and English, but was also able to take courses like politics, philosophy, and logic. In addition to the classes being more interesting than high school classes, several teachers at the college left a lasting impression on me, and most treated me with utmost respect and guided me to speak for myself. This grew my confidence in my own abilities and after a while I even started joining some extracurricular activities.

While I was at college, I wrote for the college newspaper. I worked with a team of other students, and we formed some close friendships. We were all very committed to serving the students and learning more about journalism. I enjoyed the camaraderie so much I decided to stay on the college paper even during my first year of university.

For the most part, the college paper was non-eventful, like the story and photo about the worm in the broccoli that a student had found in their meal from the cafeteria. Yuck! We also wrote about sports events and everyday happenings at the school. Maybe I shouldn't call them non-eventful, but they were everyday things that didn't have a huge impact on us. But they taught us about journalism.

One very memorable exception was an investigation into teachers who were allegedly teaching their students Marxist propaganda. The two teachers in question were definitely 'left-wing', but I never heard them trying to brainwash students to follow their politics. If anything, several of the other teachers were more likely to talk politics and praise students for voicing their opinions. The RCMP came to the college because of a complaint that several teachers were brainwashing students. Since gossip was rampant at the time, it wasn't a big surprise when an article appeared in the college newspaper with the headline "Is this Seneca College or the Red Scare?". The RCMP wouldn't provide a statement so the article noted that they wouldn't comment on the investigation.

I was the writer of that article. The article documented as much as I could learn about the investigation. It was common knowledge in the student population at that time that the two teachers were being investigated for "brainwashing" students with Marxist propaganda. I was the one on the student paper who was selected to write the article. At the time, I didn't write anything that wasn't already being talked about. Some students, including myself, were committed to communicate the truth and not just blindly let things happen around us. We took a stand by communicating this in the student newspaper. We also learned that those teachers were at risk of losing their jobs and we didn't think that was right. The students on the paper, including me, felt it was our responsibility as journalists to report the facts as much as possible and let other students know that several of their teachers may be fired because of the investigation. I think we also hoped that reporting the truth might reduce that risk of them being fired. I don't think I got a lot of co-operation from the faculty, college administration, or RCMP. I do recall a few faculty members saying it was about time the students were willing to take a stand but at no time did they try to influence or tell me what to write. As journalists, we took the matter seriously.

I don't know if the article helped the two teachers keep their job, but I did feel like we had at least made a difference.

I remember this as part of the hysteria of the 60's and 70's when communism was terrifying and the Cold War was alive and well. Some teachers at the college had left-wing political leanings, but their main goal was to get students thinking for themselves. I think they did that very well, and I always respected my instructors at college because they treated me like an adult and taught me to think for myself.

I didn't think a lot about my time on the student newspaper for many years, but when I started having PTSD symptoms, this was one of the events in my life that came back with a roaring vengeance, sometimes just as memories, and other times as flashbacks.

Throughout the worst of my PTSD symptoms, I had a horrendous fear of being called a communist and being persecuted for it, even though I have never been affiliated with any political party.

College helped me "forgive" myself by reminding me that I could think for myself and handle difficult situations. I could also stand up for things that I thought were unfair and unjust.

PTSD brought all these memories back to me in great detail decades later. All things that caused the emotion of fear or discomfort in my earlier years were brought back in the late 1990's.

I suffered from frequent flashbacks that took me back to the horrible events of my childhood and young adulthood as if they were happening all over again. I had frequent nightmares if I was able to fall sleep, and "daymares" during my waking hours. I would burst into tears for no apparent reason (to others, anyway) and my physical health was affected, including fainting, stomach issues, and high blood pressure. I had worked at a bank for several decades and some of those memories also came back to torment me.

Memories from my youth bombarded me with horrific fear. In the small town where I had lived, a young man in town was an active member of the Communist Party of Canada and a gay rights activist. He was my older brother's age and they hung around as teenagers. I don't recall any political discussions at the time, and I think this young man probably got more political when he left the small town. I thought I had seen an article in the Toronto Star, not long before my breakdown, where he was actively advocating for gay rights, contracted AIDS, and died. I'm not sure of the sequence of these events but it hit me hard that there was a "connection" between me and left-wing politics that I would be persecuted for, despite the fact that I had no involvement with many of the things for which I would be blamed. Years later, I found out that this young man (not so young anymore) was still alive. I was confused but happy to learn this.

The PTSD caused me to remember the young man and his political activism later in life. It also caused me to relate my memories to the conflict in Northern Ireland. I felt I would be blamed for the problems in Northern Ireland, and everywhere else for that matter. My fear brought me to a standstill, but I was somehow able to go on, looking over my shoulder at every move and feeling unsafe almost 24/7. Sequencing of events was almost impossible. Everything in my past that brought fear came flooding back and seemed to be happening all over again, and in the present, or so I thought. My common way of coping, not well I might add, was to try even harder to remember and tell myself how glad I was that certain things had NOT happened. One example of this was in a grocery store, I was buying some cheese and I started to tear up when I read a cheese label. I was so happy that the French translation was "fromage" rather than "rapè". If it had been "rape," I would have ended up in a heap on the grocery store floor sobbing uncontrollably.

My time at college was really the first time I related to people as an adult instead of a kid. This was the first time I felt I was accepted as a person who had valid thoughts, ideas, and feelings. My relationships, courses, and good grades at college gave me my first sense of accomplishment. It was also the first time I felt I wasn't letting my family down by giving up and quitting.

Towards the end of my time in college, I began to wonder what would come next. I had many more options now but didn't have a clear sense of what I wanted to do. I felt safe and confident at school, and my experiences there made me feel stronger. I had always considered university, and part of the reason I wanted to get my high school equivalency was because it would make me eligible. In 1976, I achieved this goal. I put myself through university by working summers at various bank branches filling in when they were short-staffed, thanks to my mother who was also in that line of work.

My years in university were probably the years I was happiest and most fulfilled. I was taking courses that interested me, and focusing on what was important to me.

I majored in History, with some focus on Political Science, philosophy, Celtic Studies, Criminology, and a few language courses; specifically French and Old Irish. My history courses included quite a few medieval history courses, but also some labour history. My focus was more on the United Kingdom since I had a real urge to learn more about my ancestral history. The culture I was most familiar with was Irish because of my grandmothers, and my aunts on my dad's side of the family. That's also the reason why I studied Celtic Studies that ranged from Old Irish to literature and history. I was able to get involved with the Celtic Arts program where I met some friends and was able to help organize events, such as music, watching classic Celtic movies, and organizing events with the Toronto Irish Players theatrical group. Storytelling and cultural events became really important to me during this time.

I had several close friends from university that I spent a lot of time with. There was also an older gentleman who was fulfilling his dream of graduating with a Bachelor of Arts. The four of us became quite good friends and stayed in touch to some extent even after graduation.

I loved going to university, learning new things, and most of all, being treated with respect and like an adult. In fact, I liked it so much that when I retired from Financial Services, I went back to a university to take courses in public administration. Many of those courses were similar to what I had previously taken, but from a different perspective. I also found it rewarding that I had a much broader perspective with decades of work experience and, of course, life behind me. Much of what I learned in my younger years made a lot more sense now.

CHAPTER FIVE

Here We Go Again!

ONE OF THE THINGS THAT ALWAYS BOTHERED ME WAS THE USE OF someone else's personal information for personal gain, especially without their consent. This is partly due to the horrendous impact it had on me while growing up. It set the stage for another sexual assault in later life when I was probably 19 or 20 years old. I remember the event in great detail.

It was at a time when I was working odds jobs to help pay for university. One of those jobs was with a man who knew my family very well. He did carpentry and home improvement jobs, and one summer I worked with him occasionally. One day, while we were working, he decided to give me some counselling on relationships. He told me my parents were concerned that I was going out with someone for the first time and they weren't sure what effect my past would have on me. I was touched that my family was aware of my vulnerability and that they took the time to make sure I would be alright, even if they hadn't asked me directly.

In retrospect, I think he lied about my parents' request. As the conversation progressed, the concern went from me to him and how his marriage wasn't fulfilling his needs. That's when I figured out something very wrong was happening. I was uncomfortable with the direction the conversation was heading and my mind wandered to dark places. His words brought me back all of a sudden: "Well, how about it?" I ended up on the floor with him removing my clothes. By the legal standards of that time, a sexual crime was not committed. I remember it happening in the mid to late 1970's and at that time, the sexual crime on the books was rape. If there was no penetration, a crime had not been committed. In 1982 Bill C-127 replaced the crime of rape with the crime of sexual assault in the *Canadian Criminal Code*. This was to address the fact that a sexual assault did not require proof of penetration and it was a crime of violence.

If that event had happened after 1982, he could have been charged with sexual assault. Assuming, of course, anyone believed me. I had been working with him and there was a pair of scissors close by. I don't remember if I actually grabbed them or if I just reached for them, but my movement startled him and he decided it would be best if I left. It never occurred to me to report an assault, and it's likely he wouldn't have been charged anyway as the "act" was never completed. I've sometimes wondered what would have happened if I had injured him with those scissors, or worse.

Unfortunately, I made the decision to spend the night at Jane's house to avoid going home after the assault. At the time, my family lived a few doors down the street from the perpetrator, so I didn't want to go home and risk seeing him again.

When I arrived at Jane's house, I was upset and confused. I called and asked if I could stay there for the night because I was afraid to go home. I don't remember talking about it that much other than I didn't want to go home that night because the perpetrator had "hit on me." The residual fear I was feeling must have been clear on my face, because when I knocked on Jane's door, she asked me if I was alright. I remember stuttering through a partial explanation, but I think Jane probably filled in some details herself.

My recollection is that we spent the evening probably doing what we often did; watching TV and chatting about life. The night was a blur and still is. I went home the next day and not a word was said about it again to Jane for many years.

The next time I heard about it from Jane is when I found out she had told my ex common law spouse, Joe, about it. She told him even before we started going out together. When I asked her why she would tell him about my sordid past, she indicated she thought she was doing me a favour by telling him so he would treat me well. I didn't buy it then, and still don't, mainly because Joe told me that she had told him all about me on our first date. He also told me what he knew about me at the time.

When I went home the day after the assault, I told my parents I wasn't going to work with the perpetrator anymore because he had "hit on me". I think my father probably would have confronted him if my mother didn't step in and explain that I was now an adult and could handle someone hitting on me. Years later when my sister found out about this, she indicated that my mother took it more seriously than she had let on, telling my sister to avoid being alone with him in the future. But for me she had little sympathy. I think it was at this time, my sister asked me if mom ever claimed she (my mother) had been assaulted as a young girl. She hadn't, and that had never really occurred to me before.

This was the first of several betrayals that I felt from a mother who should have been more inclined to protect me from these men and her church. I have never felt that my father sided with the aggressors. He was always more inclined to support me in my challenges that resulted from a person or an organization, such as the church, who were more interested in protecting their good name. There is nothing more horrific than a sexual assault when the victim is a child. Nobody understands that more than a victim who has gone through the ordeal of both the crime and the aftermath of reporting it. Our legal system, and our society, still put the victim on trial. The victim is often blamed for their own misfortune, or often seen as both aggressor and victim. After all of this, they often end up blaming themselves.

I recall my first "date" with a young musician from Belfast, Northern Ireland. He had been introduced to me by a teacher from college when he, a few classmates and I went out for an evening of Irish music. He asked my college teacher for my phone number and soon afterwards I was asked if it was alright if this information was provided. My teacher was hesitant because he didn't know if I should get involved with a musician. Our date was ironically at his band member's townhouse. We spent some time sitting on the stairs looking at Leon and Jill Uris's book, *A Terrible Beauty*. I recall it as if it were yesterday. My new friend longed for Ireland to be at peace again, and the violent conflict to be over. Many of the photos in the book portrayed his homeland during a time of peace. He eventually ended up moving back to Ireland, but I always felt he was a kindred spirit; partly because of the shared melancholy and desire for a peaceful existence.

Several years after this relationship during my university years, I met some of the people involved in Celtic music, theatre and culture. I developed friendships with several people involved in that group. I became acquainted with others including a so-called boyfriend that Jane told Joe about. After an event that ended around 1 am, I asked this acquaintance if he could drive me home. Foolishly, I thought it would be safer than taking public transit. I was sexually assaulted when he apparently thought he should be "paid" for the ride home. I didn't tell anyone about this assault because I was so ashamed and frightened. It was more violent, and I remember having scrapes up my back afterwards. He had held his hand over my mouth so I couldn't cry out. Jane was not aware of the rape and told Joe about this old 'boyfriend' despite me asking her to stop numerous times.

CHAPTER SIX

Job vs. Fulfilling Career

WHEN I GRADUATED FROM UNIVERSITY, I STARTED FULL TIME work at the bank in various positions. My previous 'part-time pool' work experience helped because I had worked in various roles that provided me the opportunity to learn most branch positions. I wasn't particularly fond of banking, but I did well, and liked the variety and chance to move around the city.

Banking was an industry where the product delivered is strictly financial, and profits were the most important goal. People, both customers and staff, were often not treated as well as I thought they should be. This changed over the years as the bank started initiatives where employee satisfaction was taken more seriously, but there were still areas where employees were treated like a commodity. Like most businesses at the time, marketing was directed at making profits rather than what customers needed or wanted. Staff was made to work ridiculous hours, sometimes without additional pay when the bank felt they could get away with it. Most branches were not unionized and bank management could impact your chance of advancement and career if they felt you were doing something they didn't like. This changed to some extent over the years, but the bottom line was always most important.

I never did excel in sales and my first posting as an authorized officer was no exception. The manager called me into her office to tell me I was being promoted at a branch on the subway line. It was only supervising two people but there were going to be personnel challenges with the two employees I'd be working with. She didn't specify those challenges but told me she was sure I could handle anything that came my way because of my good people skills. I've never liked dealing with other people's conflicts so wasn't looking forward to it.

During my tenure in this job, one of the Assistant Administration Officer roles was eliminated, so my job came to encompass the work of what was previously done by two people. It was procedure at this time for the person staying, in this case me, to go over all the data and make sure all the financials were balanced. While I was doing that, I found a $10,000 discrepancy in one of the suspense accounts that went over a period of a few days. There was clearly a mistake somewhere. I advised the Administration Officer of the branch, but he told me not to worry about it. I got the same response from the manager. At this point I was getting frustrated. It may not be a big deal to them, but it was my job to balance the accounts and these accounts were not balancing. I called head office and was also told it was only $10,000 so they wouldn't be sending anyone to take a look. I finally put it behind me, but it always stuck in my mind.

I got a rude awakening years later when that former co-worker was investigated for fraud. A previous customer had complained that he had invested money in a 5-year investment and the funds were no longer there when it matured. An internal audit was called and they went to each branch she had worked in and audited for other losses. When they called me, I told the auditor about the day I had found the discrepancy when I took over that role. The auditor, of course, told me she wouldn't tell anyone how she knew where to look, but that didn't matter to me. After the call, I went downstairs to the washroom and burst into tears. How could my co-worker do that to the people who worked with and trusted her? This was just one more in a long line of betrayals by someone I should have been able to trust, but at least she did face consequences for her actions.

After several more years in the branches, I quit because I was feeling burnt out, and was unable to transfer into a head office position. I felt my only option was to quit. I'd always had an interest in the law, so I took my LSAT and applied to several law schools. I was never accepted but it was a good experience that made me realize that I, too, could look at careers that would hold more interest for me than banking did. After getting rejected for law school I went to a private college and took courses towards becoming a paralegal (although I never pursued that career).

It wasn't long afterwards that I went back to the bank fulltime at head office. Jane told me about an opening in the Customer Information Department and suggested I should apply. I was interviewed by one of the managers of that department. It was one of the strangest interviews I ever had. To top it off, my Aunt Ida died very close to that day so I was beside myself over her death. The person who interviewed me didn't think much of the bank and didn't mince his words when he spoke to me.

I guess I made an impression on him because I got the job. He was an eccentric man, but was personable and had a good sense of humour. He also took to me because, as he put it, I was the only woman he knew who would drink Guinness beer. That wasn't exactly the claim to fame I wanted, but it would do. I'm not sure if I told him I like Guinness beer because it's not usually the kind of thing I would say at a job interview. I think it's more likely that Jane told him previously because she was a very chatty person, and apparently got to know a lot of managers in the bank, including in that department. The interview went well because we both felt comfortable chatting with each other. I was able to get across my reasons for wanting the job and sharing my qualifications. I enjoyed working with him as he was willing to share information and treated the staff, including me, with respect.

I recall telling the manager that I might not be in great form as my aunt had just passed away. He was sympathetic and compassionate. He indicated I could have delayed the interview if I wanted, but it didn't occur to me that I could do that at the time. I would have preferred it because I recall feeling numb when I heard of Aunt Ida's death. It was almost like losing my mother.

Her death affected me, partly because of her illness and the experiences I went through with her as her health declined. She had liver disease and was a heavy drinker. She'd previously been told by a doctor that she had cirrhosis of the liver. She quit drinking for a number of years and didn't consider herself an alcoholic. After a few years of sobriety, she was told by a doctor that she didn't have cirrhosis of the liver so she started drinking again. I think if she hadn't started drinking again, she would have lived a longer and healthier life. She was unable to get a liver transplant when it got to that stage in the disease. At that time, doctors would not perform a transplant on someone they considered an alcoholic because they felt it would be wasting it on someone who would just destroy it anyway. My aunt had endured a few painful years filled with illness, but she held on as long as she could and shared her wonderful passion for life with her family; especially me.

CHAPTER SEVEN

A Serious Relationship!

I T WAS AT THIS TIME THAT JANE INTRODUCED ME TO MY FUTURE common-law spouse, Joe. They had worked together for several years at the bank and had formed a friendship. Unbeknownst to me at the time, she had also told him about my past including the molestation and the fact that my neighbour had "hit on me". I will never know why she would do that although she said afterwards it was to make sure he treated me well. I don't believe that for a minute. Joe had just broken up with a previous girlfriend. I think he was still upset about the previous breakup but he seemed to move on quickly. Joe was not a demonstrative guy and, for the most part, kept his emotions to himself.

On our first date we went out for a very nice dinner at the Keg Restaurant. It was a new experience for me as I hadn't been on many formal dates. I was a little apprehensive at first, but he was pretty easy to get along with. He proceeded to tell me he'd been told all about my past by Jane. In retrospect, he didn't seem phased by the drama, but it also didn't raise any red flags for me at the time. I don't recall but I'm pretty sure he paid the bill. We frequented that restaurant during the next few years and he always paid the bill there. It was close to home and we also got to know some of the staff; especially one of the waitresses who Joe had taken a liking to. She was nice and married with a child. We became friends after a while and got to know each other a little better. When Joe and I went out it was usually for lunch or dinner at a nearby restaurant. Our alternative was watching a movie at the condominium, usually a Star Trek movie.

Things went reasonably well for the first few years, although when I look back now, we should never have gotten together. He was a tall, dark, and handsome techie who spent almost every waking hour on the computer. He was not a people person but could be very charming, friendly, and helpful. He was smart and presented himself professionally in public. He was second to none when it came to computer hardware and software and was always willing to provide technical advice or lend a helping hand when needed with technical issues. We really had nothing in common. He was conservative in his politics and often joked that I was more left-wing than him. Of course, that was true, but I'm not sure why he found it so amusing.

We didn't socialize much. We worked at the same bank, but in different departments. He was technical and I was a business analyst. We both worked in Technology and Operations, but it was a huge bank and we only worked on one project together. That project was very well run. He was the Project Manager on it, and I saw firsthand how efficient he was and how well he worked in a team. This was probably the best time we both had working in a similar field, but it went downhill quickly after the project was completed.

We knew some of the same people and usually socialized with them when we did get together with someone else. The exception to this is that Joe had been friends with several guys for quite some time, before we met. They did not work at the bank, and we socialized with them and their families. They had formed a close relationship with Joe, mainly because of their technical savvy. That's usually what they talked about. These friends were both nice, but I didn't come into the conversations much.

Joe and I went out together for several years before I moved into his condominium. The relationship had become serious quickly and we got along well. His only issue in my eyes was that he drank too much. This became a bigger issue as time went on. Initially the fact that he'd been told about my past wasn't a big issue. When Joe was not drinking, he was a nice guy to be around. As his job started to go downhill, he got home hours before I did, and had already had a few drinks. He also became very controlling and had to know where I was all the time. We rarely went out anywhere separately.

When his job at the bank started taking a turn for the worse, and he started to feel humiliated and unappreciated, he did not cope well. For the previous years, he had a good job that he liked and felt appreciated by the people he worked with, and the organization. Now he was getting projects where he felt unappreciated and disrespected. He was put in strictly technical roles with someone else managing the project, even though he'd also proven himself as a good project leader and manager. The project manager he was assigned to was making unreasonable demands, even during off-hours, and he was getting angry about it. One example was when the manager called him at home in the evening and demanded he go out in our own van and pick up supplies for the project. When Joe told him he couldn't do that, the project manager told him that it would "behoove" him to do it. Joe started feeling threatened and started drinking even more. He'd take his problems out on me. Although he said he wanted me to do well in my job, he was often jealous that my job seemed to be going well while he was being "mistreated". There was some truth to that. When he was drinking, he would blame me for everything and tell me how "fucked up" I was because I was molested as a child. He would also taunt me about old "boyfriends" that Jane had told him about. The most violent sexual assault I had experienced earlier was probably the one that I pushed back into my mind the most. Joe bringing it up in this way was very damaging and brought it to the forefront in my mind again.

Joe had been railing on me about the previous "boyfriend" who was never a boyfriend. I started feeling afraid and left. I briefly stayed with Jane, until that started to go downhill. I also stayed with my sister for a short time. Soon after I left Joe I went to live with a friend who I shared an apartment with years before. I had severe nightmares that came back with such a fierce intensity that she called my father one morning after a particularly terrifying nightmare. Apparently, she found me sobbing and rolled up into a fetal position that morning. They took me to the Emergency Department due to the nightmare and severe flashbacks that rendered me hysterical and unable to function. Years later, I would report a sexual assault for that violent rape that Joe repeatedly taunted me about to the point where I started having flashbacks about it. The horror this caused made me continuously wonder why Jane would have told him about my past in such sordid detail.

I will never understand why anyone would think gossiping like that would do anything other than hurt someone. The only thing I could think of was Jane tended to require attention and always had to be and be seen as 'in the know'. She frequently gossiped about other workmates affairs, indiscretions, illnesses, and other personal information that most prefer to keep private, or at least have the opportunity to tell their own story to those they entrust with this information; especially in a work environment.

In retrospect, I know Jane's gossip and the constant reminders from Joe had an extremely negative impact on me. I had spent years putting my violent past to the back of my mind. Now those who should have been closest to me were throwing it in my face any time they got frustrated or angry. Memories I'd tried so hard to repress for decades were rearing their ugly head again.

My fear about Jane's gossip was now at a critical level and I was afraid for my job, my reputation, and even my life. The fear for my life wasn't a result of Jane's gossip but from the PTSD symptoms. Jane terrified me, but I was afraid to call her out because I thought she would get angrier and just gossip more about me. She could get verbally aggressive, and I felt she was already angry at me for breaking up with Joe. I was also afraid she would ruin the reputation of some other people I worked with who didn't deserve her wrath. I was pretty sure I was going to die, and probably a violent death. I had recurring thoughts that one of my previous attackers or one of their friends would come to the bank and kill me. I think this was due to the many intrusive memories of past assaults, and the flashbacks.

I also had a fear that my previous spouse would kill me. I was having flashbacks of the two times that he veered our vehicle towards a cement bridge on a highway while saying he was going to "take us both out." I was also remembering the time he told me how easy it would be to stab your spouse to death. Deep down, I didn't think he would hurt me, but there was always the possibility that he would. I never talked to anyone about that until I started getting professional help to cope with the PTSD. This was a terrifying time of my life, and it affected me for years. Quite honestly, it still does. To this day, I won't put a block of kitchen knives in full view because they're a reminder of this terrifying time in my life.

CHAPTER EIGHT

Work & Home Environments. No Peaceful Haven.

M Y WORK ENVIRONMENT CONSISTED OF WHAT PEOPLE THOUGHT was a big happy work family where everyone got along. That was partially true for a while, but once a few people felt "privileged" enough, they thought they could walk over others and use the relationship they had built with the Vice President of the area. Sadly, they could. The claws came out and the work environment got very toxic, especially for me.

I was never very competitive although I could usually hold my own if necessary. That was true until home life also became difficult, and in some cases, dangerous. A few of the women who wanted to get ahead started setting me up for failure. It confused me because I would always be doing the jobs they didn't even want. I could have understood if they wanted my job, but they didn't. Truthfully, my job wasn't that great, and it was certainly not glamorous. At the time, I thought they wanted me to fail and look stupid in order to make them look good and indispensable. Even now, I don't think I was wrong to feel that way, as such toxic work environments make people do things they wouldn't normally do. It certainly makes many people think of nobody but themselves. One thing I learned very quickly was that nobody who worked there was indispensable.

Things became extremely personal, ranging from indiscriminate talk about personal serious health issues to sex lives. I became the "bitch" when I sat with a few of the women in the cafeteria for lunch one day. Jane couldn't accept the fact I was trying to ease the tension by sitting with them in the cafeteria. Instead, she laughed and said to me, "What a bitch." If there was a person that I wish I had never met, Jane was that person.

A new Project Manager came into the area. She was a nice enough woman, but some things she said made me uncomfortable. One of the first questions she asked me was if my mother died from breast cancer. To make it worse, she seemed disappointed when I replied my mother died from non-Hodgkin's Lymphoma. CIBC's Run for the Cure was, and still is, a huge fundraiser that the bank has supported for years. I remember being upset that my mother had died from the wrong type of cancer at the time, silly as that might sound.

She also asked me out of the blue, "how would you feel to have a man's hands all over your body?" Where did that come from? It was not something you usually heard in a professional environment, especially from someone you didn't know well. Comments like that would send my brain reeling with memories flooding back.

Even people who were previously supportive were now acting differently towards me. By that time, I was suffering from PTSD symptoms, but certainly not enough for me to be making up the actions of my fellow workers. Several were actively sabotaging my success, and others who had some control over my success were ignoring me and throwing insinuations around. My boss was staying away from me as much as possible so a few of my colleagues wouldn't see me with him. He, too, had to have heard some of the insinuations.

The most damaging insinuation was that I was having a relationship with a former boss. This was not true. I felt like I was back in high school with Jane, a nemesis by that point, trying to "protect" me from the other people I worked with. One example was when my boss and I had to go to a meeting together. We met in his office. The administrative assistant who sat beside him, smirked and told us how cute we looked together. She was also the same person who insinuated affairs with a few of the men she previously or currently worked with, including our resource manager. I'll write a little more about her shortly. I was so incredibly uncomfortable I also avoided people that I really needed to communicate with frequently to do my job well.

One of the other women would be jealous if I spoke to our boss. She often stated that he liked me better than her. I have no idea if this was true because he treated everyone fairly and respectfully. I do think he was intimidated with the relationship several of the women in our area had with his boss, the Vice President, because they were known to run to her any time a male manager would say something they took offence to. The one that stuck in my mind was when a co-worker died. We had a new project manager appointed right at the time of her death. He sent us a message with the funeral details and told us to "feel free" to attend the funeral. One of the women was so upset that he used the words "feel free" that she stormed into the Vice President's office to complain.

My home life was also tense since Joe was unhappy with his job, and often jealous that I seemed to be doing well. Only one of us was allowed to be stressed out at home, and that, of course, was not me because his job and happiness was more important than mine. I don't think there was a day he didn't have at least a few or more drinks to rid himself of his daily stresses. When I mentioned it, it would result in an argument. When I mentioned it the next day, he claimed he didn't remember the argument. Or at least that's what he would tell me.

From the start of our relationship, he always told me he'd never see the age of 40. He thought he'd be dead from a heart attack before that. He was also very money conscious. I think that was what he valued most in life; that and Star Trek. Throughout our relationship, I watched every Star Trek movie and every episode of every Star Trek series. I was never a big Star Trek fan but he sure was. I think the reason this stuck in my mind is that when we both worked at the same bank, they put on a skit with several V.P.'s as Star Trek characters to address some of the cultural changes being made in the work environment. One Vice President was Jean-Luc Picard, and our area's Vice President was Captain Janeway. My common-law spouse's reaction was "it's about time". He told me if the bank could follow some of the guiding principles of Star Trek they might be on the right path. Well, that didn't happen and his career didn't go the way he envisioned. I often felt that a downward spiral began when something that was supposed to be a guiding light in your life suddenly turned bad and turned your life upside down. This was certainly the case in my past.

Around this time, we also got the new contract employee who took over as the administrative assistant. She soon made it known that she was personal friends with Fidel Castro, was capable of putting hexes on people, and often insinuated closer relationships with co-workers. She was strange but friendly at first. After a while she started wearing different clothes, which would be fine in and of itself, but got creepy when she told us that she only wore that clothing when she was putting a hex on someone.

One of the most disturbing instances was when she told us she took a pencil out of her manager's office so she'd have something she touched (which was necessary to put a hex on her). She indicated she didn't want to kill her, only to make her life miserable. I can't remember her exact words but they were either to make her manager's life "miserable" or a "living hell". Either way it wasn't good.

Another event that really bothered me was when she cooed and cawed when I went to a meeting with my boss. She went on about how cute we looked together. I think this had such an impact on me because Joe frequently insinuated that my boss and I were meant for each other. I would bristle whenever I saw a truck (a special events company, I believe) that had "An Exclusive Affair" painted on the side of it. When I was working at the bank, trucks for this company appeared often, or so it seemed to me at the time. I worried Joe would become convinced I was having an affair. My sense of danger increased greatly and I found it necessary to stay away from my boss, and almost every male I worked with. During that time, another jealous co-worker often told me that my boss liked me better than her. I couldn't go into his office without these insinuations from both of them. It was high school all over again.

When I had my "crash and burn" episode the first time at work, I mentioned to my boss that I couldn't work in these conditions anymore. I mentioned our administrative assistant and that she was acting in a threatening manner towards others. He was aware of some of the weird stories she was telling but wouldn't have realized the impact it was having on me. My first "crash and burn" included me going to the nurse's office at work because my anxiety was so high that I couldn't function. I had an asthma attack around that time as well. Jane told my boss where I was, and they both came to the nurse's office. The two of them sat with me for a while and we chatted. I remember wishing Jane would leave because she never stopped talking and I needed some silence to gather the thoughts swirling in my head. My director sent me home in a cab and told me to take a few weeks off to regain my health. The administrative assistant's contract was not renewed.

There was a time afterwards that I was sure our administrative assistant had put a hex on me just as she said she did on her boss. This time, I was sure, she wouldn't be concerned if her "victim" died. My sense of danger increased because an ongoing joke in the area was that the Resource Manager was in the Mafia. He was actually a nice guy and never did anything that would indicate any indiscretions and certainly no sense of danger. It was only because he was Italian, and part of the Resource Centre, that this "joke" ever came to be. The Resource Centre was part of the Human Resources area that assigned employees to various projects and were often just seen as a bureaucratic hindrance. It was still new to the bank and even the Resource Managers were unsure of their roles. The joke was that they could hold a project hostage either by giving us experienced resources, or just someone to fill a role. Training was important, of course, but tight timelines for projects often required highly experienced resources and minimal time spent training people in new technology. Either way, I was sure the administrative assistant knew it was me that ended her employment in our area and possibly the bank. I was sure she would be just as happy to see me dead.

It was almost killing me, at least psychologically. My ability to block out or at least dull the memories of the things that terrified me was broken and I didn't know how to fix it. In my more peaceful moments, I knew these things were in my past, but the intensity and strong emotion that went along with these flashbacks and intrusive memories were very real and present. It was only when the flashbacks subsided that I could comprehend they were in the past and I was reasonably safe. My sense of safety was badly damaged and any hope of feeling safe at home or work at the time was gone.

As a result, the most difficult thing to do was to learn to trust my own judgment again. It's one thing when other people might think something is wrong with you. It's quite another when you have lost the ability to trust yourself. It takes a tremendous amount of time, support and concentration to put your thoughts back in the correct 'folders' of your mind so you can begin to trust your perception of the world again. Even though you might still be able to function well on the outside, the inner turmoil is almost too much to bear.

Working in Operations and Technology at a bank was both a curse and a blessing during the time when my PTSD symptoms were at their worst. My exposure to technology, the detail-oriented job I had, and the precise planning that goes into the testing and implementation of a technology project was a godsend. It helped me separate the intense emotion I was feeling with the more practical reality I was experiencing at the time. My ability to "block" the turmoil was back, at least partly, but it took a real effort and was exhausting.

I was having intrusive thoughts of the previous assaults and was afraid my attackers would come to my workplace. I would rationalize that even if they did, they would not be able to get into the building because they would have to go through security. This provided some peace of mind, but was still disturbing and exhausting. At the same time, it was in the back of my mind that two of my attackers were ministers, and therefore trustworthy to most people. The other was a head-hunter; again, a profession that came into play at a time when the bank was reorganizing and job security was probably at an all-time low.

I would sometimes see someone who reminded me of one of my attackers and become paralyzed with fear. I don't recall feeling that my life was really in danger at that point, but I was afraid of another sexual assault. I was afraid to tell anyone because I thought I was losing my mind and they wouldn't believe I had ever been assaulted anyway. I was also afraid that if I told Jane, who was supposed to be my friend and support system at that time, she would blab it all over my workplace. I would feel like an even bigger target for the gossip and cruelty of some of my co-workers. I was also afraid she would tell Joe, who constantly threw my past in my face. Jane had handed him the original verbal weapons, some of them incorrect information. The only thing I felt I could do was remain silent and hope it would stop. It almost killed me.

My experience in risk management also affected my thinking at the time because I spent many hours thinking about the "what-ifs" and analyzing possible consequences. Most of those consequences were negative, resulting in either the death of someone close to me, or myself. I think my job equipped me to rationalize some of the risks and make some sense of them. I was often convinced that my job skills were going to kill me, but it was also the thing that was helping me survive. Post-traumatic stress is absolutely rife with contradiction.

Another factor that weighed heavily on my mind was my family. They had already been through the trauma of someone close to them surviving an assault and I didn't want them to go through that experience again. They were there with me again during my recovery, but it was something I tried to protect them from the best I could.

During the worst of the PTSD symptoms, every time I saw a familiar name at the bank it was like going back in time, either because the person was someone my mother knew when she worked there years before, or it was someone I had worked with. Fortunately, many of these memories were reasonably good but every now and then an event where I felt threatened would surface. These often consisted of an event where I or a staff member was actually threatened, or a hold up where there was the threat of violence. I would also flash back to the time when one branch was frequently under surveillance because of the number of times we were held up. Ironically, that was one of the times I felt safest because I felt the police were close by and could take action if anyone attacked me. It was strange that the feeling I was being watched could actually be comforting.

My thought at the time was that the people watching over me were the good guys and the bad guys wanted me dead. It was like an internal fight between good and evil. I was able to convince myself that the good guys were watching me. They would somehow figure out what was true from all of the information they were hearing about me. I was suffering from paranoia, but they would be watching over me and prevent the bad guys from harming me. Things seemed either really good or really bad to me all the time. There was little middle ground, if any. Things would either help me survive (good) or let me die (evil). I thought the good guys who were watching me would see through the lies and know them for what they were. The lies being spread would become clear and everything would be alright; if only I could survive just a little bit longer.

I was petrified that I hadn't reported two sexual assaults, and people who didn't know would send the rapists to where I was, and it would happen all over again. I was petrified to report the crimes, and equally petrified not to report them. As a result, I was paralyzed. I would pray that it would all fall into place so my family and I would be safe. At this time, I thought I was losing my mind. During some of these times, I knew what I was "remembering" was in the past; not current, but it all seemed real and present. It was difficult to distinguish what was real and current, and what was either a flashback or vivid memory. Either way it was extremely disturbing.

CHAPTER NINE

Shattered Patterns

I'M NOT XENA, WARRIOR PRINCESS. APPARENTLY, THE PROJECT Manager told the rest of the implementation team that I was the area's Xena on the fateful day in October, 1997 when I finally came crashing down. This was my second crash and burn. The warrior princess who I hadn't recognized in me before this, had helped bring the project to the day when it could be implemented. I was a Business Consultant on the project once it got to the testing and implementation phase. My knowledge of testing and implementation and the working relationships I had established over the years with the people who would actually implement the project were incredibly important to the overall project. I just hadn't recognized it at the time.

I recall absolute terror when a co-worker who was trying to show that she was in charge came up behind me while I was working at the computer. She kept asking me, "Where's your list?" I assumed she was referring to a list of functions that she thought I personally was going to check. We had never discussed it, so I felt extremely intimidated and I froze. Funny thing is, I know the testers who were present on that day did have a list of functions to verify in the live system. They also had test cases to verify in the live system and were very capable of performing their jobs. My co-worker would have known this because the implementation would have been discussed in previous meetings. I still think to this day that she deliberately wanted to antagonize me.

The next thing I recall was leaning up against a wall with my head hung down and a manager from another unit, who was coordinating the actual implementation, asking me if I was alright. I told him I thought I should be in the hospital. He got my Project Manager who guided me into a nearby office for privacy. We chatted for a while. I recall talking to the Project Manager and, I think, giving a fairly coherent and eloquent speech asking why we couldn't all get along. He presumably called my sister to pick me up and take me to the hospital. He then led me downstairs to an office near our own unit so people wouldn't be walking by and I would have more privacy. A few of the guys I worked with dropped into the room where I was at that time to make sure I was safe. It seemed like forever but probably wasn't a long time. The walls were closing in around me and I had no idea where I was or what was happening. I recall two co-workers coming in to make sure I was alright. I had a conversation with one of them who I felt was a kindred spirit, as he, too, had been through a lot of very difficult times recently with the death of his wife and sister in a terrible accident. The other co-worker was very supportive but I remember the only thing I said to him was, "It's terrible being used."

My sister, her husband and new baby came and picked me up to take me to the hospital not long afterwards. I have no recollection of how many hours had gone by, but it seemed like an eternity. I went to the Emergency Department to get checked out and went home the same day.

My concept of time was non-existent. The intense emotion, mistrust, and connections I was making at that time were often absurd. When I look back at it now, I understand how my past could create such a horror story, sometimes a conspiracy theory, and always an intense dread that something terrible was going to happen. Many events I experienced or witnessed that brought on the extreme emotion and fear of violence came rushing back. Everything 'happened' at once in my reality with the intense emotion of the actual events that had happened years before.

Words mean much more when you are experiencing symptoms of PTSD. They take on multiple meanings and can cause horrific thoughts, memories, and stress. Technology is rife with words with a militaristic meaning. The internet was created by the US Military based on their knowledge of the human brain. I think they were right in most of their findings but, man, what horror that can cause.

COLT was and probably still is the major banks' financial transaction system. It's also the name of a gun maker. Conversion of data is one of the things I worked on most during my tenure in the Customer Information Department. This also brought back memories of violence against me at church in my childhood. Mergers and acquisitions brought on new meaning and put thoughts of a hostile take-over in my mind. During this time there was talk of two major banks merging; including the one where I worked. There had previously been a brain-drain from one to the other. My feeling was this was not a coincidence but was all intentional and it scared me.

It also crossed over to my earlier years as a history student. The term 'Republican' meant Irish Republican to me, not a right wing American political party. The term 'Unionist' to me at that time meant Ulster Protestant; not a labour union movement. Opposite meanings led me to believe people with power were making decisions on incorrect information, and false beliefs. The potential outcomes terrified me. Labour also meant giving birth; not the labour movement. I felt the people I was working with were confusing this and faulting me for being unsupportive of the women in my area with children. This was far from the truth. I, always willingly, and without complaint, came into work on the weekends so they could be home with their children. When one of them needed a business consultation on something I was more experienced with, I dropped everything to meet them and stayed later to do my own work. I think this is why I felt so betrayed by my co-workers. I can't remember a time when I felt I was being used by my co-workers at Head Office until then. I was distraught that they would see me as a bitch who didn't support them at work.

Or worse, they knew I was providing the support they requested and just didn't care. It was never enough.

MY HOMELAND AT WAR?!

∞

My educational background was in history and some of that history was personal to me. It wasn't just something I had read in a book or learned in class. Much of what I learned about my family history, and Canadian involvement in world events, such as the world wars, came from first-hand stories.

In my family there were several veterans of war. One was very active in the Legion and recounted many war stories to me as I was growing up; especially in the later years of his life. He was also friends with my cousin, another veteran who was very active in the Legion. Their wives were best of friends and had been for many years. My cousin was from Great Britain and worked in the insurance industry. I didn't know him well but remember him from family gatherings. Another uncle rarely spoke about the war. He was meek and mild and chose to forget that part of his life, although he did frequent the Legion to play pool, cards and indulge in a few beers. The only story I recall him telling me of the war years was when he was deployed in France. He told me he got to eat horse meat and it was really good. He wished Canadians also ate horse meat.

Funny the memories we have and share. Family war stories also included one of my mom's brothers. He was killed in action during World War II. In my mid-teens, my uncle who worked at the Legion brought over the couple who were the custodians of the War Cemetery in the Netherlands where my uncle is buried. It brought feelings of sadness that he died at such a young age, and pride that he was being remembered with love by many who didn't even know him. I often wondered what he would have been like had he returned from the war.

I discovered the history of Ireland through formal education, but also significantly from stories I heard from friends and family who were directly affected by The Troubles in Northern Ireland and the news I read about the issues. I learned the history of World War II from history books, but also from first-hand stories I heard from my uncles who were personally involved in fighting in the war.

When I first experienced my symptoms of PTSD I would think back to those stories of war and civil unrest. I would think how horrific they must have been and consider my past traumas, such as the assaults, and symptoms of post-traumatic stress less significant, in comparison to what other people had been through. I understand now that trauma affects people differently.

Comparing traumas is damaging, especially when we minimize our own. I felt I should have been able to cope better and not let them impact me as much. My most severe symptoms made me feel like I was at war, or at least as much as I could possibly understand what that would be like. One of my uncles, who had fought in World War II, had told occasional stories about it when I was younger. He didn't dwell on it when we talked and didn't tell vivid stories about battles, but the pain and fear he had experienced came through in his words anyway. Now that I was experiencing my PTSD symptoms, I began to think often of my uncle and his stories. I found myself relating to him and his experiences more than I related to people who had lived experiences more like my own.

I was embarrassed and often felt guilty that I related better with someone who had been through a war. I didn't think I deserved it and wasn't that brave. I think, at the time, I was grasping at straws to understand what was happening to me and his was an experience that sounded similar. My knowledge of PTSD at the time was also extremely limited because mental health awareness had not yet reached the mainstream, so for me PTSD existed in the context of shell shock, battle fatigue, and experiences related to war. I had never been at war literally and had a difficult time comprehending what was happening.

After a while, stories of the Irish conflict and WWII were invading my waking hours and my sleep. Loud noises reminded me of gunfire or bombs blasting. I had nightmares of carnage and people dying in a war zone. I never thought it possible that I could experience such intense feelings about something I had not been directly involved in, but it felt very real to me.

Equally terrifying, I was experiencing intrusive memories of past wars, and flashbacks of the assaults that had been perpetrated against me. These memories and flashbacks were intertwined in my mind and felt related, even though they weren't in reality. My sense of timing and historical sequencing of events was really out of whack. The memories of wars and flashbacks of assaults were all getting mixed up as something that was very recent and very real. The stories of past wars and conflicts brought back the same intense emotions as my own assaults. The stories of my uncle's involvement in WWII and the conflict in Northern Ireland were more disturbing to me than my own stories of past assaults because they were much "bigger" than my own experience and impacted more people.

My feelings of horror and helplessness impacted my perception of the world and made me feel very inconsequential. Even the most mundane things began to affect me in terrible ways. The red hand on a flashing pedestrian walkway reminded me of the Red Hand of Ulster, a symbol used by Protestants in the Irish conflict, and I was paralyzed with fear thinking the troubles of Northern Ireland had come to Canada. This fear eventually morphed into a fear of traffic lights generally, and traffic lights were everywhere. At work during the Year 2000 project, we even used traffic light colours to signify the readiness of an application in becoming Year 2000 compliant (green for ready, yellow indicated outstanding issues, and red meant additional work was required).

Wallpaper was another mundane thing that triggered me and also reflected my pattern of confusing images and times to meld together. I had decorated my bedroom when I was in my early twenties with wallpaper with the pattern name, Columbine. The design was an elfin pen and ink type drawings in brown and beige. It was in this small apartment near some relatives in Toronto where

I lived and first felt independent and mature. I chose that wallpaper because it made me feel peaceful and calm. But for some reason, I remembered it in a childhood room. It was never in my childhood bedroom, only the room I had when I was in my twenties. Human memory is fallible, of course, but this lapse was troubling. Decades divided the reality from the facts.

The pattern name was also significant because I later spent years working in an area that focused on name and address information. Names were significant to me. PTSD symptoms brought back memories of everything that was named Columbine; the wallpaper, the flower, the horrific high school shooting in the US.

I had a doctor once when I was younger, a caring woman, who told me that sometimes when a child experiences abuse, they have the ability to 'disappear' into the wallpaper to escape the assault. I don't remember if I disappeared into the wallpaper while I was being assaulted as a child, but my trauma and confusion surrounding the wallpaper made sense when I remembered back to what the doctor told me.

Another significant fear for me was that I would be persecuted by some of my extended family for having a relationship with someone of a different faith. My knowledge of the conflict in Northern Ireland was reasonably good as I had studied and researched those events in university history classes. This sometimes paralyzed me with fear because my first consensual relationship was with a young Catholic man from Belfast, Northern Ireland. It also brought back memories of my cousin deciding to go to a Catholic Church with her daughter; knowing her father was a staunch Protestant. I often wondered if she did that because she really wanted to learn about the faith, and teach her daughter tolerance, or if she just wanted to annoy her father. I remembered another uncle asking me one day if I thought that was why she did it too. I really hope not because to me, the intermingling of politics and religion was manipulative and disingenuous. It corrupted the purpose of spirituality, which to me, had been so badly damaged by the earlier assaults, and stole away that spirituality for a time. To me, spirituality (and religion) was something that should bring peace and comfort; not conflict and pain.

And then things progressed even more. The 6 o'clock news became my backyard. I had worked at the bank dealing with names and addresses every day. The doctor who brought me into this world and later became my gynecologist had the same last name as a US President. A big mouth co-worker who had previously brought me grief at my first management post had the same last name of a prominent US military person. As I previously mentioned, a childhood friend had the same last name as a prominent American involved in security. Needless to say, those big names in the news in the U.S. at the time, and also a big part of my past, did not always bring forth the best of memories. Many of these absurd conspiracy theories were occurring to me during the horrors of 9-11. During that time, I was working on a high stress project that enabled customers to access their accounts on the internet in real time and send funds to another person's account. Thankfully it was only within Canada at the time with a relatively small daily limit, but it did still cause me considerable grief thinking of how horrible it would be if I was enabling terrorists to send funds easily through the internet.

My fear of the PTSD symptoms and being attacked again during the years I was having the worst symptoms shattered my world perspective – physically, emotionally, and spiritually. This went on for several years until I had undergone intense professional help. I had long held the idea that the histories I knew so well – the battles, plots, bombings, and genocides – were in the past. They had happened, they were real, and there were significant consequences, both to individuals and to the world as a whole, but we had learned from them. We knew better now. We understood each other better, and we were determined to work out our issues in a civilized manner; not fall to pieces and revert to violence like we had in the past. The next large-scale conflict would be resolved without so much bloodshed. But now, because of my symptoms, I no longer believed the horrific was impossible. I, personally, had recently experienced at home and work, how cruel people can be to each other. My perspective and worldview had changed and I no longer believed we were safe. I just waited for the horrific to happen again. I was sure it would happen again. And for some reason, I thought I should be able to stop whatever it was.

During this time, I knew my past was terrorizing me but I didn't know how to stop it. I experienced intense false memories of war and terrorist events; things that felt real to me in the moment but that I knew I had never actually experienced first-hand. I was sure these events were going to happen again, and the death and destruction would be worse than the first time around.

TREATMENT

These vivid memories, coupled with flashbacks were so intense that I thought I was losing my mind, although deep down I knew most of what I was reliving was real and had happened. This contradiction was wreaking havoc on my concept of reality, and I had a very difficult time coping with it. I was so relieved when the flashbacks became less frequent and eventually stopped after much professional treatment. I also wished that my memory of them had gone away. Those memories haven't gone away even now, but I can explain what was happening and they no longer terrify me the way they did when they were flashbacks and vivid memories.

The professional treatment I received was varied. It started with several visits to the Emergency Department of two nearby hospitals; one in October and the other was the following January. The first emergency doctor checked my vital signs and sent me home. The next emergency doctor was also rushed and spent little time with me. The solution at the time was medication. The second emergency doctor was a psychiatrist and at least knew the medications that were available, but he didn't spend any time to diagnose me. In fact, he didn't even try. That being said, the medication did make me feel more human and allow me to sleep again. One of the worst symptoms of PTSD for me was the inability to sleep. The second doctor also referred me to a counsellor at the hospital, so I had someone to talk to.

She gave me some wonderful tips, like journaling, to ease the stress. Our conversations didn't start off well because once I told her my story, her reaction was "oh, you poor woman". I recoiled and refused to see myself as a victim, even though at that time, I was. I didn't need someone to pity me. I needed someone to stand beside me and bring out the strengths that had helped me survive up to this point. I spoke to her several times and she did help. It was just never the kind of professional relationship that could have brought me to a place of self-confidence and strength again. I felt like she pitied me and saw me as weak. This may not have been true, but to me, it was. I went in to speak to her for several months and also stayed on the prescribed medication for about 6 months. Both helped but I didn't feel I would get much better at that point.

I went to see the psychiatrist one more time as a follow up to my second visit to the emergency department. He told me I had experienced acute depression. I don't recall much more than that other than speaking to him briefly about the trauma and the fear that I had when I was with Joe. I recall him asking me if I didn't think it was normal to have intimate relationships with a man you were living with. I recall telling him that it was, but not when I didn't want to. I think he agreed at that point that I had been traumatized. Another thing that I recall from that appointment was my warped sense of humour. I think it has saved me several times, but it really threw me for a while. When the doctor told me I had experienced acute depression, I remember my first reaction was, "That's easy for you to say. It sure wasn't cute to me." I don't think I said it out loud, but I remember it vividly.

I eventually went to speak to several people at work who were responsible for the staff and provided or organized leadership courses and training. I told them the issues I was facing. One of them recommended a psychologist who specialized in trauma therapy. This was probably 4 or 5 years after I first started experiencing some of the worst symptoms. I maintained a professional relationship with that psychologist for over 20 years, and in fact, still keep in touch.

Her treatments and my trust in her is what I needed to get through the post-traumatic stress and all the confusion I had been experiencing. I also learned the tremendous impact those experiences had on me. Initially, we just talked and talked and talked. I did most of the talking, of course. After I had regained enough strength again, she tried EMDR Therapy (Eye Movement Desensitization and Reprocessing). We reframed the traumas so I wouldn't keep blaming myself for the assaults. The EMDR was difficult because it did bring back a lot of the painful experiences, but by this time, I felt I was safe with her, so it was helpful. I had remembered most of the assaults before, but this gave them clarity and helped me process the pain that I had felt. I did talk therapy and EMDR for several years and was eventually able to increase the amount of time between appointments. I recall them being weekly, then bi-weekly, eventually monthly and finally several times a year just to check in and make sure all was fine. My coping skills were pretty good again, and I had confidence in my ability to cope. That was a very big deal.

My recovery was really dependant on all of the treatments that I received during that time; from the medication, to the suggestion of journaling, to the talk therapy and EMDR. The journaling and talk therapy also reminded me to not dwell on the negative things, but to make a point of remembering and acknowledging at least three good things every day. I did this no matter how difficult it was, even if it was something like seeing a flower bloom that brought me a sense of peace.

Journaling also helped me get negative thoughts out of my system, much as if I had talked to someone about them. It helped me create that narrative of my story instead of memories coming back in snippets. The narrative brought some sense to my life and helped me understand it better.

Once I was more comfortable and not feeling as paranoid and unsafe, I made a point to go for walks to places that I had been before and meant something to me. For example, I visited my old college and university to refamiliarize myself with them. Much had changed, of course, but there was a lot that I was able to recall. This increased my self-confidence and took away the fear that I was going crazy, or at least, losing my memory.

I've learned a lot about my mental health, and I make a point to speak to a professional and monitor my own level of stress. It has made a big difference because one of the things that scared me for years was that I would experience the horrific symptoms of PTSD again. I didn't think I would survive another episode like the first and was determined to take my mental health seriously.

I went years with talk therapy and was able to cope well with a stressful life and job. I did re-experience a setback after many years when my second career took a turn for the worse. I was involved in the mental health initiatives in the organization where I worked. This gave me some meaning, and a feeling that what I had gone through wasn't all for naught. When my co-workers started to cause my stress to rise again, I re-experienced some of the same symptoms, but not as intensely. I did have one more visit to an emergency room, but I was able to take myself there and speak to the doctor myself in a fairly coherent manner. I was put on medication again and had to readjust my work environment so I was able to concentrate enough to do my job. I was able to work from home and stay away from the people who were causing my anxiety. Eventually I was able to retire and start putting words to paper in this memoir. My desire was always to communicate this journey of mine so others might understand their own stresses, or those of their loved ones better.

My psychologist hesitated from giving me an official diagnosis of PTSD. I've always wanted to thank her for that because I think if she had, I might have ended my life not wanting to live in a war zone. It was only after I learned more about my own mental health that I asked her. By that time, I had been working in a profession that was very active in learning more about PTSD and learning to provide better support in a high stress environment. She acknowledged that I had been treated for PTSD symptoms and recovered. That was what I needed to hear. I was told I would always have to be cognizant of my stress level and know that my risk level for stress was high. As for the severe PTS symptoms, those memories had been reprocessed. I would never experience PTS symptoms of those events again as severely as I had. I was good with that and will always make a point to treat my mental health as well as, or even better, than I do with my physical health.

With all the confusion in my mind at the time, I was petrified of a diagnosis of PTSD. I only related it to combat so, at that time, it would have meant to me that Canada was literally at war. I didn't want that to be possible, and certainly never wanted that to be my reality. As a result, I convinced myself I could not have PTSD. It was just me battling the demons of my past. I now know that what I experienced was severe PTSD symptoms. I've often felt, and sometimes said, that what I experienced was similar to what a soldier or first responder might experience if they had PTSD; only the content of the nightmares and flashbacks was different. I'm not an expert in psychology and the symptoms of PTSD, but this does make sense to me now and explains some of the triggers and memories that troubled me all through this ordeal. The memories were mostly of war and conflict. The triggers were things that reminded me of the assaults. From my own understanding of PTSD, I think what I was experiencing was acute, cumulative, and vicarious trauma for a period of time where both my own traumas and those of others close to me were magnified and wreaked havoc.

Past memories of events one of my family members experienced came back to me. One example of this is when my father was a police officer. He didn't often come home and tell us about the horrible things he had to deal with, but I recall several incidents in particular. One of them was a plane crash that happened in Toronto. Police officers from around the province were asked to assist with the ordeal and clean-up of the site. I remember knowing that my father was one of the officers who did go to assist. He never told us anything about it but I read about the crash in the news and learned what a horrific site it was. My PTSD symptoms many years after that incident, brought it all back to the point where I had visions of bodies on the ground and first responders picking up the pieces in horror.

That knowledge and awareness of the trauma that others experienced had a big impact on me and caused some of the same emotions as it might have during the actual experiences. This was true in my personal history and in the broader history that I learned in university and life.

A RISING TIDE LIFTS ALL BOATS

∞

Given long-time conditioning and stigma associated with mental health issues, it's not surprising that few people talk about PTSD or their experiences with it. As a result, most people with PTSD suffer in silence and their loved ones are left struggling to understand. There are few resources available and little understanding about the subject and its impact.

In staying mute, we deprive ourselves of the value in supporting each other on the path to recovery and success. Today, with the rise of recognition about mental health and its impact, we're finally seeing a corresponding recognition that a rising tide lifts all boats. We all benefit when we get more intentional about inspiring, uplifting, and elevating others dealing with mental health issues (including PTSD). In so doing, we elevate ourselves. Sharing opens unexpected opportunities to benefit all.

Coming from a place of grace, generosity, and service has profound positive benefits for the giver. As noted by Alex Hermozi, author of *$100M Offers*, "People who help others (with zero expectation) experience higher levels of fulfillment, live longer, and make more money."

With that philosophy in mind, he posed this simple question to his readers:

Would you help someone you've never met, if it didn't cost you money, but you never got credit for it?

I'd like to echo that question for you to consider.

I'm on a mission to help those experiencing PTSD to get more of what they want and deserve in life through greater understanding. To achieve that goal, I need to reach them. To reach them, they need to discover this book. One sure-fire way to increase the likelihood of them finding it is through reviews. So, here's my ask. If you think this book would benefit others dealing with PTSD, please take a moment now to leave a review. It costs nothing but a moment of your time.

That review might help another person coping with PTSD …

♦ Find peace

♦ Get the resources they deserve

♦ Improve their relationships

♦ Rediscover their life

Think of the power your simple review wields. A moment of your time could change a life.

Share the gift of empowerment. Thanks for considering this!

CHAPTER TEN

Painful Past and Haunting Memories

THE POST-TRAUMATIC STRESS SYMPTOMS THAT I EXPERIENCED were worse than the actual assaults because of the overwhelming fear and inability to shut out the horrible images, and even physical pain to some extent. We usually have a defense mechanism that allows us to cope with the horrific. Mine was broken and not available to me. The assaults had a finite timeline, but the post-traumatic stress symptoms brought those same emotions and horror back for a much longer period of time. The impacts lasted much longer than the initial events.

In the past I had frequently found myself blocking out the pain when things got too difficult, but now that defense mechanism of dissociation was no longer there to assist me through the most painful times. My ability to dissociate, even temporarily, was no longer an option for me, even when it was necessary for survival. PTS symptoms took that defense mechanism away from me.

It was like the file folders of my mind got tossed into the wind and the pieces of information were sometimes put back in the wrong place. My experience in technology made me think that my relational database, as it were, was out of whack. A relational database is one that recognizes the relationships between stored pieces of information. It's part of my technology background that helped me explain what I was going through at the time. My mind was putting every piece of information together, rather than in a way that I could make sense of it. I doubt that an individual could have caused an international incident from their past, but I felt that I could, or at least, I would be blamed for everything bad that happened.

Any time the slippery slope got too dangerous I was very glad that I had a psychologist I could talk to and remind me I wasn't crazy.

Acronyms can also be a curse if you're experiencing PTSD symptoms. For example, in a banking technology and operations work environment, I was thinking both IRA (Investment Retirement Account, Irish Republican Army) when I came into contact with a trigger that made me think of the conflict in Ireland. My knowledge of financial products and my education in the history of Ireland crossed over and became terrifying to me. That created a very real fear that somebody was going to be killed. I didn't always think I would be the person killed, but often a family member or friend. I was also thinking that the world, and more specifically my family, would be better off without me. This fear was very real to me as I did have knowledge of Irish politics and had friends and family on both sides of The Troubles. The scariest thing was that

I didn't know who or what side of the conflict was going to strike the deadly blow. I felt unsafe with both sides of the conflict in Northern Ireland and felt that either side could have been the death of me.

Many of my memories were a desperate attempt to put some sanity to my past and explain what was happening to me. I was remembering nonsensical things (or so I thought) in an effort to create a narrative of my history. I was remembering things that terrified me first and explained things second. This ranged from real, personal events, to things I had learned, read or seen on television (especially the news). Memories of television shows or movies came rushing back in my mind, mainly those that depicted violence. One that came back frequently was Don Johnson in *Ceasefire*. I repeatedly had a vivid recollection of the scenes where he was flashing back to the Vietnam War. It was brutal, but I felt that this was what I was going through; not the Vietnam War obviously, but my own war with the violence in my past, both in reality and in what I learned from others over the years. Ironically, in that movie, his flashbacks to the Vietnam War occurred in his children's playground in the backyard.

Throughout this time, Jane responded to me with anger and hostility. Her response to my pain was asking if I was satisfied that she, too, was molested as a child. I didn't understand why she would bring this up in this way. Why would her pain make me happy?

That was the first time that Jane had ever mentioned that she, too, had been assaulted as a child. Because of my own experience, I felt guilty and had to believe that she was telling the truth. I didn't understand, and still don't, why she hadn't told me before when we talked about my experiences of past assaults. Especially since she was so willing to talk to others, including at work, about my assaults. It made no sense to me and I was incredibly hurt. To top it off, it was during the first week after I had left Joe. I had gone to Jane and her husband's home immediately after leaving Joe so I had a safe place to stay temporarily. Jane and I had gone out for a walk and ended up in a nearby park sitting on a swing. We were sitting on the swing chatting and she told me of her assault; quite angrily as if her experience was more important and destructive than mine.

I don't recall much before or after that now, other than sitting on the swing in bewilderment wondering what had just happened. I recall the two of us sitting there, looking at each other, and soon afterwards walking back to Jane's. That exchange (or anything about her assault) was never mentioned again. We remained friends for a while afterwards, but soon drifted apart. My reaction was similar to what it was for most of our years as friends. I didn't call. She didn't call. I assume, perhaps incorrectly, that she may even still think we're friends. As for me, our friendship ended probably within the next few years when I decided never to reach out to her again because our friendship felt very one-sided. Oddly, she may think the same way.

My friendship with Jane wasn't my only relationship that suffered during this time either. Joe was still struggling at work, and it seemed like the worse it got for him, the more he came to resent me. He began dropping little hints about violence. This began to feel more sinister one night when we were watching the news. There had been a murder in our home town; a husband had stabbed his wife to death. I recall Joe saying how easy it would be to do that. I don't remember feeling threatened at the time he said it because it was so matter of fact. But as things in our relationship started to deteriorate, that comment came back to me. I would think about it while I was trying to fall asleep at night, and eventually even when things were good between us, I couldn't banish the words from my mind. This was the beginning of the end of our relationship.

During our last few months together, we both had difficulty sleeping; him because he was angry with his work situation, and me because I was afraid of him. He would get up, go to the kitchen, and get a glass of wine. Then he'd sit in front of the computer for hours. Every time he got up, I woke up too and I'd follow him into the hallway. I needed to know where he was. The first thing I would see was the block of Cutco knives sitting on the counter, and I would wonder how on earth I could protect myself if he decided to come at me with one of them. There were many times I wanted to hide those knives, but I was always afraid to. If the thought of stabbing me to death hadn't crossed his mind before, my moving that block of knives certainly would have brought it to his attention. As a result, they just sat there and my anxiety got worse and worse. It was at that point I actually thought having a gun in the house might not be so bad. Joe had always wanted to move to Texas and said he would get a gun if we did. I always dreaded that, but when the possibility of death by stabbing became more of a possibility in my mind, I thought the gunfire would be less messy and not quite as shocking to whoever found my body.

I don't know how likely it was that the image in my head would become reality. Joe didn't threaten to kill me with a gun. He didn't hold a knife to my throat or threaten to hit me, and his innocuous little comments about violence were rarely geared towards me alone. Instead, he seemed to enjoy the idea of taking us both out. The first incident was on our way to work one morning. He said that he was thinking of driving into a cement bridge pillar. I was afraid but said nothing. The morning was similar to every other morning and we were driving in to his office along the highway. When we arrived, I would then take the subway up to my office. At the time, I blamed myself for overreacting, even though I don't recall responding to him in a frightened way; just a little shocked. I was extremely anxious for the rest of the drive, but, as usual, probably didn't appear that way to him. I remember him smiling afterwards and not mentioning it again. I recall me thinking he may have thought it was funny, but I sure didn't.

After that incident, I always wanted to take public transit into work rather than driving with him to his office. He would have nothing to do with it, usually with an excuse of the added cost associated with taking two public transit systems. I wasn't strong enough at the time, or was too afraid, to push it any further and sat on pins and needles as we drove into work every morning. I had thought of it as a one-off incident, but apparently it wasn't.

The next time he threatened me with our vehicle was the day of my first collapse at work. My boss had sent me home in a taxi, and Joe was waiting for me at home. He said he wanted to go out for lunch. I felt terrible and stressed but I felt it would be easier on me if I just went. By that time, I was afraid of him and didn't want to refuse and start a fight. I was also still numb from my collapse at work and didn't feel capable to do much of anything. I'm not sure what I thought would happen if we argued about it, but I was sure I didn't have it in me at that time.

That day, he decided he wanted to try out the new toll highway. On the way there he drove pretty fast, and I remember feeling like I was in a trance. I was there but didn't feel present. The numbness from work was still strong and I barely knew where I was or what was happening. For all I knew, I could have been sitting at home on the couch. Suddenly, Joe swerved towards a cement bridge pillar and said he "could take us both out". I remember screaming, putting my head down and covering my face so I couldn't see what was happening. It was sheer terror and I was sure that was the end of us both, literally! I don't remember much about the remainder of the ride to the restaurant but he straightened out the vehicle again and we continued in silence. My trance deepened and I recall very little about lunch other than taking it home because I couldn't eat.

The rest of that day was strange for me and later that evening, I packed a few things and called a taxi. My destination was Jane's house, where I planned to stay for a few days and pull myself together. As I was preparing to leave, Joe stopped me. He asked me why I was afraid of him. I think earlier in the day he had mentioned that Jane would be on his side. He often said he had poor taste in women and this was the second time he had a relationship with a left-wing woman. Not sure where that came from, as we didn't often discuss politics. He asked me if he had ever hit me. I remember wishing at that time that he would so I wouldn't feel guilty leaving. I recall him giving me the "I told you so" comment that I would leave him soon. I recall him standing in my way at the door so I couldn't pass him. He put his arms around me to hold me back. I started crying and I'm sure he could tell I was afraid. He finally moved over so I could leave. As I was walking out, he brought up my boss again and said that my boss and I were meant for each other. I remember the numbness still and standing in the lobby crying while I was waiting for the cab. The condo security guard and anyone walking by must have wondered what was wrong with me, but nobody said a word.

When I got to Jane's house she was talking to Joe on the phone. When the door opened, she was still on the phone with him. It must have been a cordless or her husband may have opened the door; not sure which. She soon hung up and told me that it was him she had been talking to. She laughed and mentioned that he thought I was wasting his money, yet again, by taking the cab to her place. I think she was amused by that. I must have looked a mess, because I still have very little recollection of the drive over in the cab, my arrival and the hours afterwards. I remember feeling exhausted and still numb.

I'd been concerned previously that Joe was going to harm himself. My mind recalled the two previous incidents with the vehicle. I called one of Joe's friends as soon as I found his phone number that same night so he could check on him to make sure he was alright. His friend's first words to me were "have you left him?", so I don't think my leaving him came as a surprise.

My following days at Jane's are a blur, but I recall meeting Boris, the spider in their downstairs bathroom. Yes, they actually named a spider that frequented the bathroom, and I, for one, was terrified of spiders. That fear has subsided to some extent, but not entirely.

Jane's spouse was a tall man who was very quiet, funny at times, and unassuming. I thought he was a good match for her because he was a calming influence and a little more serious and common sensical. When I arrived at their home, I recall him shrugging to her indicating he didn't know what he should do, but he was still calming, even to me. They had been married years before. I was the only non-family member that attended their wedding at Jane's family farm. The three of us sometimes got together and talked about the good old days, and music. I had known Jane's spouse as long as she did because they met in a bar in Toronto when some of us got together to celebrate a birthday. Jane and I were sharing an apartment at the time, so I got to know her spouse fairly well when he would come to visit her. Neither one of them made me feel like the third wheel at the time and I was grateful for that. We were friends and I was very happy for Jane and wished her nothing but the best in their life together.

On my arrival though, Jane's husband was at a loss, not knowing what to say or do. I never had any hard feelings toward her spouse, but instead, felt sorry that he had a wife who gossiped a lot about his family; especially his brother who also had some health concerns.

While I was with Joe, I wasn't usually afraid that he would kill me, but it was certainly in the back of my mind.

It's strange how these thoughts play on your mind for years. It was more than ten years later before I could put a block of kitchen knives on the kitchen counter. Before that, every time I saw a block of knives it took me back to that time when I was afraid that I was going to be stabbed to death. Even now they're tucked away a bit so my glance doesn't go there first.

When Joe and I finally split up, he did show signs of violence. He killed our pet rabbit, apparently by giving it a bath in boiling water. He phoned me and told me to come over and clean up the mess. I declined. Later, he trashed the apartment and broke many of my things, his big screen TV, and a grandmother clock he had bought years before that had sentimental value. He had bought that clock with money he received when his grandmother passed away. Again, he called and told me to come over and clean up the mess. This time I relented. I was concerned for his well-being, so I called my father and he accompanied me to the old apartment.

We knocked when we arrived, but no one answered. I still had a key, so I let us in through the front door. There was no immediate sign of Joe. The place was a mess. My father was looking around at the mess he'd made, at what my ex had done. As I picked through the apartment, I thought to myself that I was glad I had left when I did.

We found Joe lying in bed. He seemed more or less alright, but at that time, I was concerned he would do something to hurt himself. No matter what our circumstances were, I didn't want any harm to come to him. While I cleaned up the living room as best I could, my father talked to Joe. Then we left.

Later I felt guilty for asking my father to go with me because it occurred to me that if Joe had wanted to hurt me, he probably wouldn't have thought twice about hurting my father as well. When he called and told me to come over and clean up a mess, he told me I better not tell anyone where I was going or bring anyone with me. I also felt guilty asking my dad to come with me as he should have been able to retire in peace without doing things for his eldest daughter when perhaps I should have called a uniformed police officer.

BANK SECURITY COMPROMISED?

∞

Another of my stressors was a few disturbing practices from our Human Resources Department. During this time, my PTSD symptoms wreaked havoc and really impacted my perception of life.

I felt that I was deliberately targeted by our Management, in part because of the past childhood sexual assaults. This was the case both at work and on a larger scale. I felt as if I were a human lab rat with people pushing the buttons they knew would cause me pain. I thought Joe and Jane were involved in this. I also felt a few other workmates, friends, and in a few cases, extended family members were pushing my buttons. To me at that time, Human Resources Department was also obviously involved. This became more evident when I got my severance package from the bank signed by a woman with my maternal grandmother's name. Another name I saw in Human Resources was a woman with Jane's mother's name. I've never been a big believer in coincidence, at least not on this scale where absolutely everything seemed to form a pattern. It was very weird to me.

MY PERSONAL SPACE - TESTED AND AT WAR

∞

One of the most disturbing patterns that occurred during the worst of the non-violent PTSD symptoms was a result of my background, my working mostly in Testing and Technical Service environments and the intimate knowledge I had of the bank's test environments, including the data. It was like the data in those test environments was copied and sent to a software company specializing in customer and household information warehousing. Acronyms were also problematic to me because they often stood for contradictory things. One of the realities in the bank at that time was many of the subsidiary companies had a smaller infrastructure system or were PC-based. They didn't understand or care about the complexities of the larger infrastructure systems and the timelines were usually very unrealistic. My tortured perception at the time felt that someone had copied the data and sent it to a prominent business for analysis and marketing. This was causing a huge problem for me because of the personal information that was often used for testing. Some was disguised so the real person wasn't at risk but there were times when production data was used and the real and disguised information was mixed together. Many test cases had coded names due to my previous co-worker, but some of the information in the body of the record, i.e., mother's maiden name, was not always disguised. This also happened to be a field that was used as a security question as not many people know another person's mother's maiden name.

When I looked at the website of that prominent business, I also found out that one of the users of their software was the US government. I don't know what specific software, but it terrified me that information was being used for security testing and there was a jumble of real and unreal information. It also terrified me that the US banks were not as regulated as in Canada and the software was often used more for marketing purposes and had less stringent matching criteria. This concerned me because of a high potential that data would be brought together when, in fact, it was not related in any way. Does this sounds familiar?

To me, it was similar to how my brain was working at the time where events and information were mixed together. At the bank where I worked, this software and customer data was used for marketing purposes, but was also used for data integrity purposes, such as consolidating duplicate customer records. A different software program was used for household information, but I was not as familiar and didn't really work with that particular software. It was less specific than the consolidation software that dealt with individual customer information, rather than members of the same household. At the worst of my symptoms the customer matching software was geared more towards a bank or financial institution, and the householding software was geared more towards an insurance company. This later became problematic to me when an insurance agent came to my new hometown to question me about Joe.

This relationship between banking and insurance came back to haunt me. Joe had been in a vehicle accident and was suing due to an impaired driving accident in which he claimed both drivers were impaired. Years before, Joe and a woman, who I understood to be a girlfriend called me. The girlfriend wanted to know why Joe and I split and if Joe was ever mean to me. He had been in a car accident and apparently was acting a little erratic due to a head injury. I had no idea what was really going on. Afterwards, I wished I hadn't talked to them about it at all.

My experience with insurance companies also became problematic to me when I had an unpleasant encounter with a cousin who graciously tried to get me a job in his old insurance agency. I turned it down because I wouldn't have made enough to even pay my rent. The sound of the job also did not give me a good feeling and I was pretty sure I wouldn't like the job. Rather than accepting it and quitting, I turned it down.

Ironically, I worked for a time in an insurance agent's office years later. I was further convinced that banks had a little more going for them than insurance companies in how they treated people. In all fairness, the women who worked in that insurance office did provide good customer service to the clients when they could, but the office environment was very toxic to me. The women in the office had also put a picture of naked men from the movie, *The Full Monty*, with hats strategically to hide their genitals. Every time I went into the washroom and saw it, I was uncomfortable but afraid to ask them to take it down. It reminded me of the bank again, and I was frightened.

In retrospect, I think the only reason I was hired was because the insurance agent wanted to pump me for information and use my background to grow his investment business within his agency. He was a card-carrying member of a major political party. I've never been in an office where my politics and knowledge of banking was under such scrutiny, or at least that's how I felt. We rarely discussed insurance.

The horror of 9/11 was also magnified for me because my manager at the time was from Manhattan. I learned about the attack from a co-worker. She phoned me around 11 a.m. from another location and asked me if I knew what had happened. I didn't. All I had heard was the guys from Internet Banking talking about a plane colliding into the World Trade Centre. I thought they were playing a video game on a break since this was sometimes what happened when there was a lot going on. Our head office was evacuated just in case and we were given the option to go home and be with our family. We had a meeting scheduled at head office that afternoon and I stayed to make sure everyone knew it was cancelled. I remember feeling very unimportant because I didn't have anyone to go home to. Most others lived with family and had children who I thought needed their parents to explain what the world had just experienced. My own world was very small at the time and I felt I was of little consequence. To top it off, I was working on a project that would allow customers to send funds through the internet with a direct link to the bank's financial infrastructure. If that wasn't the stupidest thing to do after the World Trade Centre had just been attacked, I didn't know what was. I didn't have anyone to go home to as I lived alone. I stayed at work until mid-afternoon and then went home and watched it over and over and over again on TV. I made myself a music CD to deal with the sadness I felt and the overall horror that something like that could happen. Some of the music, especially the lyrics made me cry uncontrollably; but they also brought comfort and an eerie peaceful calm.

UNDER INVESTIGATION

∞

During much of this time, I was pretty sure I was under investigation for something, but I didn't know what. I had left Joe and my mind was on overdrive almost constantly; even when I was asleep. It crossed my mind many times that my university days were back to haunt me and the RCMP thought I was a political dissident, partly because of my Irish/Romanian background, partly because I used to work on the college newspaper, and partly because I used to hang around the Irish Cultural Centre.

That being said, I felt that way mainly because I was now persona non grata at the bank and several co-workers had it in for me, including at least one with an executive position. Those who used to talk to me, now ignored me when they saw me coming towards them. Others who would talk to me only did so if they needed something or if they needed my input on a project they were working on.

I had moved into an apartment closer to my workplace and had my own space. I finally felt I was living my own life without people constantly telling me what to do. When I moved, certain things caught my eye in my surroundings. I vividly remember a beige Intrepid that often parked across the street. I felt safer when it was there because I thought I was being watched. For some reason, the Intrepid made me feel as safe as I could at the time. That was the time I felt I was being watched or under surveillance by the good guys. I was feeling paranoid at that time and felt that if the bad guys came to hurt or kill me, whoever owned that beige Intrepid would be there to protect me. It made absolutely no sense, but it was a coping mechanism to help me feel safer. I also knew I had done nothing wrong so had no fear at all of being under surveillance.

Several names triggered fear during that time of paranoia. They brought back the days when I went to college because one of the teachers who was under investigation for allegedly brainwashing students with Marxist propaganda had the same last name as the VP of the area I worked in at the bank. Many of my issues were because of her. I felt she was targeting me for not joining her weekend get togethers. She also minimized the horror I went through when I originally had the breakdown. I wouldn't be the least surprised if she put some of her friends (my co-workers) up to making my life miserable. I'm pretty sure she made my boss transfer me out of the area not long after I came back to work. I was transferred into the worst possible area for me at that time in Testing and Technical Services. The VP tried to come across as if she was there for me, but in reality, she did not provide support for people who worked for her unless they asked "how high?" when she asked them to jump. The people close to her knew she would support them no matter what at my expense.

Those who were previously good for me to work with avoided me as much as possible so they weren't seen with me. I'm pretty sure they knew I was in her bad book and didn't want to jeopardize their own job. I don't blame them for that, but under the circumstances, they should have stepped in and stopped the persecution. Several of them knew my situation had reached a dangerous level and my life was potentially in danger. I felt terribly betrayed and alone with only the reassuring possibility that someone was watching over me, and I had done nothing wrong to deserve this.

Ironically, this was the same feeling I had when I travelled to Northern Ireland with my aunt and uncle in 2002. When a British army vehicle was being driven right in front of us, a soldier was pointing a gun directly at us. I felt surrealistically safe because I knew I had done nothing wrong. Post-traumatic stress symptoms bring the ironies of life to the forefront and sometimes make life surreal.

MY TRIP TO IRELAND

I had always wanted to go to Ireland. I had applied to several universities when I was younger so I could study in the land that I wanted to know more about. I had applied to Queen's University, Belfast, Northern Ireland and University College, Dublin in the 1970's. I don't recall the reasons but I never did go to Ireland then, but studied in my hometown of Toronto. In retrospect, that was probably the best thing to do as Northern Ireland was in turmoil. I don't remember hearing back from either university, but Toronto is a wonderful place to learn as well.

In 2001, my aunt advised me she and my uncle were going to Ireland for a 3-week vacation. She asked me if I was interested in going with them. My first reaction was, wow, what a chance of a lifetime and I responded that I would. The planning was a little strange. My aunt suggested we stay in Bed & Breakfast locations for our vacation and that we could share a room. I loved the idea of Bed & Breakfast locations so we could meet more people and immerse ourselves more in the everyday way of life. I'm not one to share rooms and insisted that I would have my own room. That was fine, and possibly even preferable to all concerned. I didn't feel close enough to share a room, especially with my uncle. We didn't book our locations before we went but would plan as we travelled depending on the time of day and how we felt. We stayed for several days in a few places.

Our vacation consisted of two weeks in the Republic of Ireland and one week in Northern Ireland. My uncle still had family in Northern Ireland and we visited with them. They were nice people who had adjusted well to all they had experienced over the years. His one aunt had an older house on a fair size piece of property with nice flower gardens. It really struck a chord with me when I went into her home and saw walls full of clocks. Over the years, she had accumulated a huge number of clocks. It was quite impressive.

During our vacation we saw many of the sites I'd heard of over the years. There were a few that we didn't go to, including the Blarney Stone. My uncle asked me if I was set on seeing the Blarney Stone but I told him there was quite enough blarney in Canada already. For those of you who don't know, blarney is the gift of the gab where it is said that the Irish have an uncanny ability to persuade and charm people with flattery. It would have been nice to see everything, but we had limited time.

The scenery was amazing and reminded me a little of Eastern Canada with the plush green fields, the rugged coastline and the ocean. One thing that surprised me was the trees. There were quite a few palm trees on the coast of Ireland. I had heard there were palm trees in Cork on the south of the island, but there were also some in places further north. There were also monkey puzzle trees that were an evergreen that I had never seen before. These intrigued me with their uniqueness and beauty. We travelled through some small coastal towns and saw the ships and sailboats. It was beautiful.

The most intriguing and surreal places we visited were sites I recalled from Irish history classes in university and research I had done as a history student. I had taken Celtic Studies courses and learned much of the folklore of Ireland, poetry and medieval historical sites. Being there in person brought back those days in a very surreal way. I often felt like I was in a trance and travelling back in time. One of the most surreal places I visited was Trinity College in Dublin where I saw some of the old Irish manuscripts that I had learned about years earlier.

All in all, my vacation to Ireland was a wish come true for something that I'd wanted for decades. My aunt and uncle are staunch Christians and don't drink other than for communion. I had told my aunt before I would not go to Ireland if I didn't have a half pint of real Guinness. That would be okay in her eyes and we smiled at each other and started looking forward to a wonderful vacation. I had never been on a vacation with them before and was a little apprehensive because I knew my uncle had very strong feelings and views of his home country, Northern Ireland. Nevertheless, we got along alright and I felt this could be overlooked to see the beauty and feel the culture of a land I had wanted to visit for a very long time.

For the most part, the vacation was wonderful. There were a few times when I felt under attack by my uncle when he went out of his way to visit places that would remind him of Protestant victory and superiority. More important to me, I felt he was going out of his way to let me know the Protestants won the battle. One of those days was the day that almost ruined the whole vacation for me. He had made a point of stopping a young lady, and, I presume, her daughter on their way to a Catholic Church. He asked them for directions to the site of the Battle of the Boyne, the site where William of Orange, in 1690, fought with the deposed English King James II. William of Orange and his wife had acceded to the Crowns of England and Scotland the previous year after the deposition of the Catholic James II. James, through an alliance with France attempted to retake his throne. William's victory on the shores of the River

Boyne was the conflict that ultimately ensured the ascendancy of the Protestant factions in Ireland that would last for centuries; until the Republic of Ireland was given independence from Britain in 1921, with the exception of Northern Ireland which to this day is still part of the United Kingdom.

Back to my story, we drove in the direction that was given to find the site of the Battle of the Boyne. A funny thing about Ireland is that some of the directional road signs point in opposite directions but presumably go to the same place. I, apparently, had been appointed navigator. We never did make it to the site of the Battle of the Boyne, and my uncle stopped at least once to fume and fret about it. He must have known I was agitated, and so was my aunt. He was driving like a bit of a mad man in my view and I was actually afraid. He must have sensed this because I recall him telling me that he didn't blame me that we never found our desired location. That was the evening when we stopped at a local pub for dinner around 10 pm. I told my aunt I was going to have that half pint of Guinness. She urged me to have a whole pint, and I did!

I find it hard to explain how I felt on that vacation. I was intrigued and in awe of visiting the places in person that I had learned about. I think the PTSD symptoms almost numbed me in a few instances where I felt I was outside of my body looking on as a spectator. I felt peaceful, yet sometimes unsafe. Looking back now, it was a very surreal vacation. It's time to go back for a visit when I can do some of the things that attract me to Ireland so much; like listening to Celtic music and visit a few places that I didn't get to see the first time.

I think my favourite and most peaceful part of the vacation was the one day we spent in Dublin just before coming home. I took a bus trip around the city by myself to see some of the places I had heard about and learned the history. Dublin is a beautiful city with wonderful parks, the Liffey River and history galore. During the bus tour, the driver explained the sites with an Irish lilt and sang Irish songs in between stories. I felt some heartbreak at the sites where I know violence had taken place and people were killed. But overall, the tour was magical and I recall feeling at peace during most moments.

I came back to Canada with a newfound knowledge of my ancestral homeland and, of course, some wonderful reminders of the trip that I still have today. I gave some away but kept a few special memories, and lots of photos. Several weeks after returning to work, I was offered an early retirement package to leave the bank. I happily and immediately, but with a few tears, accepted it and started my life over again.

CHAPTER ELEVEN

The Split & the Breakthrough - And Jesus Wept

T HE THING THAT BOTHERED AND FRIGHTENED ME MOST WAS THE memory loss. I was petrified that my usually good memory was lost and gone forever. When I think of it, memory loss might not be the right way to describe it. My memory wasn't really lost. It was just so jumbled and the sequencing of my past was so far out of whack that I couldn't make sense of it. The confusion was unreal. Simple things like adding and subtracting were difficult for me because I didn't have the concentration for even the simplest of mathematics. This hit me especially hard because I excelled at math in school and spent much of my adult life working in a bank. As you can imagine, there are a lot of numbers in that line of work.

Something that struck me even harder is that memories of the childhood assaults came back as if it were yesterday. As I struggled with my memory, I tried desperately to remember even a few bible verses that my molester had taught me as a child. The only fragment I could remember was "Jesus Wept". I looked it up in a St. James Version of the Holy Bible and was so upset that I didn't even get that right. It was "And Jesus Wept". I'm sure on that day, he did.

I was questioning my spirituality constantly. I often went back to a time when others judged me and criticized me, sometimes silently, for not going to church any more. I never completely lost my spirituality although I certainly questioned the teachings of organized religion. When I was going through the worst of my symptoms, the one saving grace that I could rely on was that I had not lost or sold my soul to the devil. But it had been mercilessly snatched from me! I was paying a very high price for the horrific deeds of others and the cover-up that followed to ensure the high esteem of a religious organization was not sullied.

Fortunately, I was eventually able to slow the confusion in my mind and regain much of my memory in a proper sequence. I could remember some of the verses; not ones that I learned on those fateful days, but as a child going to church with a loving and supportive family who did their best to live a good life and instill the values of integrity, respect, truthfulness, and kindness in their children. But still, I was immensely triggered.

One of the things I did to help face my fears was to go to a church to see what my response would be. It was several years after my initial breakthrough and I had received some therapy to help me cope with the PTS symptoms. The church I chose to attend was within walking distance of my apartment and I hoped it was a progressive and non-judgemental church where I would feel comfortable enough to listen to some of the hymns that I heard as a child. It was more difficult than I ever thought it would be. During much of the service, I sat in the pew with tears streaming down my face but too embarrassed to get up and leave because people would see me crying. I sat through the whole service. When I went to leave, the pastor welcomed me to her church and the tears started to flow again. I spoke to her in her office afterwards and explained why I was there. She was a very understanding woman and I went back to speak to her a few times afterwards. At that time in my journey, religion wasn't what I needed, but this experience did allay some of my fears.

Another thing that really threw me for a loop was the utter confusion and a tendency to think in terms of good and evil, positive and negative, and in opposite extremes. Nothing was easy and absolutely everything meant something. Most things had several meanings, and sometimes hidden meanings. It took an excruciating amount of thought to make sense of it.

As I mentioned before, I see my memory as thoughts stored in folders to organize them, to put things into context, and to make sense of the facts and feelings of experience. The stress I was experiencing had thrown the folders of my memory open and absolutely wreaked havoc with my mind. I was remembering people from my past. Most events and people from my past seemed as if they were in the here and now. I was trying to make sense and rationalize what was happening; not to justify, but to explain.

I tried hard to ease the pain by remembering something good that could somehow balance the really horrific. One example of this, strangely, was the Oklahoma bombing. I'm not sure what triggered that memory but it brought back the horror of seeing it on the news years before. It brought back memories of several friends I went to college with who happened to have the same last name as the bomber. I remembered these two friends in contrast, and somehow was able to get the vivid pictures that I had seen on the news about the bombing out of my head.

CHAPTER TWELVE

A Dance with the Devil

I WAS HAVING A REAL INTERNAL BATTLE WITH MY SPIRITUALITY. I was afraid to be Christian because two of my attackers were ministers and most of my worst memories were in a religious setting. Much of my family are practising Christians and are wonderful people who epitomize what it means to be a good Christian. I felt that some of my extended family was more supportive and sympathetic to my attackers than they were to me. I still feel this is true. Others in my family think the ability to forgive is the ultimate proof you are a Christian. There is no doubt in my mind that forgiveness is healing, especially for the victim. But I think in their misguided way, they also became the judge as to whether you truly forgave. It also meant that you should just forget the fact that something very wrong has happened to you. If the memories still impact you, they saw it as a sign that you haven't forgiven someone. Your ability to forgive and be a good Christian comes into question. This is par for the course in a society that still tends to protect the guilty and minimize the victim. I found it so distressing that my own extended family were often the worst ones to blame me when it came down to something so horrific.

MOTHERS ARE FOREVER!

My mother and I always had a good relationship, even through my rebellious teenage years. My only regret is not discussing my feelings toward the assault with her in more detail. This was partly me, and also her, as she didn't find it easy to discuss difficult personal matters.

Mom and I spent hours playing board games, and to some extent, discussing our similar work situations as we both worked at the bank for years. In my adult years, we got along wonderfully and were good friends. Her illness and death were a huge blow to my family, and to me personally. I took it really hard though people may not have recognized it until much later. By that time, I was very good at hiding my emotion. Like my mother, I came across as a strong woman who could put her own feelings aside when necessary and look at things objectively. Mom was definitely more assertive than I was though, and let her opinions be known more than I did. She often told me this was because she was the youngest of twelve children and had to speak out to be heard every now and then.

Our close relationship had a big impact on me and became more evident at her funeral.

This concept of forgiveness came up at my mother's funeral. One of the ministers who had known my family for years also knew my first attacker. I don't think he'd been aware of it at the time it happened but was made aware of it some years later. When my mother died, he was one of several ministers who officiated at her funeral. He took it upon himself to portray my mother's Christianity by the way she was able to forgive even the most horrific of acts. I'm sure this was in reference to me and the fact I had been assaulted many years before. My mother and I didn't see eye to eye on how I should respond to the assault. I found out at my mother's funeral that she was able to forgive the man who assaulted her daughter; and by doing so proved her humanity and her Christianity to the congregation.

It was strange when I discussed this event at my mother's funeral because several people responded the same way I did. I recall my father touching my arm in support when the pastor brought it up. A childhood friend spoke to me after the funeral service and was concerned because she also thought the pastor was referring to the assault against me when he mentioned my mother's ability to forgive. My brother indicated to me that it made him angry that he would bring that up, but anger was easier to deal with than the sadness that followed my mother's death. My brother is one of the least angry people I know, but he also doesn't like to show a lot of emotion, so I certainly understood the way he felt.

I'm not angry that my mother forgave my attacker because what he did affected my whole family. I was taken aback at such a reference at my mother's funeral and felt it was unfair and targeted me, partly because I no longer went to church. It was difficult enough to deal with my mother's death, the circus of her funeral with her extended family in the quiet room (that was ironically very noisy) and the intense emotion that went with that. The last thing I needed to be reminded of during that time was my assault.

It was disturbing to learn that all was well and forgiven, at least according to my deceased mother. Forgiveness had washed away the evil deeds. I might sound angry as I write about this, but I'm not really. It was more disappointment. I think it's important that anyone who provides support, emotionally and spiritually, shouldn't get bogged down with the concept of forgiveness. It is important to forgive to get past the hurt and the anger, but it's most important to allow a person to heal and acknowledge that forgiveness does not, in any way, minimize what happened in the past. And it's also important to acknowledge that someone else cannot forgive on your behalf. I don't think the pastor meant to make me feel bad, but he could have used better judgment providing support to a grieving family in their time of bereavement.

My mother's belief in forgiveness was a big influence on how I learned this concept and played a big part in my healing. I am, in part, able to forgive because of her influence, and am also able to advocate because of both parent's strong belief in justice and fairness, especially when it involved a personal assault on someone's sense of safety.

It's strange to me how I often felt guilty for not feeling "angry enough". Anger wasn't and isn't an easy emotion for me to deal with whether it's my own anger or that of somebody else.

MEETING MY FIRST ATTACKER AGAIN!

∞

Years after mom's funeral, I contacted one of the ministers who led her service so I could get in touch with my attacker and meet with him to discuss the past. I don't recall mentioning my mother's funeral to him and didn't feel that was important to discuss. I had been told years earlier he would help me get in touch with the man from my past that I now needed to reintroduce myself to in order to move forward.

I got in touch with my attacker for several reasons. First and foremost, it was the only way I thought I could stop the flashbacks, and the resulting upheaval I was going through. Flashbacks take you back to the event in a very intense way. I thought I would probably recognize him if I saw him but didn't trust my judgment because so many years had passed, and my mind was in turmoil because of the PTSD symptoms. I second-guessed myself constantly, feeling like any man I saw could be him. But rationally, I knew this was not the case. I convinced myself I might be incorrect to think he was a really big man who reminded me of Frankenstein because of his stature and flat head. That was the way I remembered him from my childhood. I thought the only way I could get over this was to actually see him.

Another reason was to deal with the last and most serious argument I ever had with my mother. I had refused to meet with him years earlier and she thought I should have. It was basically the "forgive and get over it" speech. Thirdly, it was almost a self-test to see how much I remembered, and more importantly to see if I would fall apart all over again. To me, this was probably one of my actions that I questioned the most and wondered if I had really lost my mind. This was something that I had to do.

I arranged to fly out west to stay with family for a week. I coordinated for my brother and I to meet my attacker for lunch at a fairly quiet local restaurant. As soon as the man stepped out of his car, I knew exactly who he was. He looked like an older version of the man I remembered vividly. I recall letting him read a letter I had written to him, so I didn't actually have to say the words. He gave it back to me after he read it. He apologized and explained some of what happened afterwards.

One of the most disturbing things was that his stepfather and a few other peers in the Evangelical Baptist Fellowship apparently convinced him to go back into the ministry. He explained that he was nervous going back into it because he didn't want to be in a position where an assault could happen again, but he did return after being convinced.

We said a few more words about the event, chatted about our lives a bit, and ate. I recall ordering a shrimp sandwich because I didn't want either him or my brother to order the same thing I was going to be eating. It sounds strange, but I think it was my effort to differentiate myself from everyone else and because I didn't want my brother to have to go through any of the same things I did.

Afterwards, my assaulter gave me a copy of a book he had written. Silly me asked him to sign it and he signed it, "here's to a renewed friendship".

The reunion with the aging pastor was somewhat surreal and creepy, but I think it was a good thing for me to do at the time. It proved to me that my recollection of that part of my history was accurate, and that I would not fall apart when confronted with it again. It proved to me that I had, in fact, made some peace with my past. I was able to move forward with my life and keep the bad memories in that one folder of my past.

Years after the assault, but years before I went to meet him, he wanted to get a higher position in the Fellowship. At that time, he met with my parents to apologize for what he had done. He asked them to arrange a meeting with me as well, but I declined. I assumed he probably wanted to get together to avoid charges or a lawsuit. It was around the same time the media was writing a lot about the Christian Brothers' child abuse issues in Newfoundland. I spoke to my father about it who advised me this probably wasn't the case, because he had already been charged and convicted in my case.

Years after my mother's death and my meeting with my attacker, I went to have lunch with a missionary couple who had known my family for years and were very good friends with my aunt and uncle. They were a very nice couple. He and I had a conversation about what had happened and it was then I learned my attacker had met with my parents because he was thinking of running for the Presidency of the Baptist Fellowship (not sure exactly what it was called.) It was felt at the time he had to deal with his past demons to run for such a position, and there was also gossip at the time about what had happened. I remember a friend from Toronto, who didn't know my family when the assaults took place, asking about it because she had heard some gossip.

Anyway, the conversation with me was about how lucky my attacker was that he'd been convinced not to run for the presidency because of his past conviction. The missionary was also a former convict who had been saved and joined the ministry and became a missionary. He was definitely a reformed person and I had no misgivings about him at all, other than the fact that this conversation led me to believe he, too, like all the others, was more concerned about the Institution than the victims of numerous assaults. Apparently, my father had talked to him and told him there was no way a convicted child molester should be considered for that position and that he would take action to prevent it, including going to the media if necessary. The missionary was more concerned with protecting the reputation of the Fellowship.

I have some understanding of people who hold on to religious dogma so tightly that they feel threatened if there's any questioning of those beliefs and institutions. I certainly don't agree with it. I've often thought of the amount of child abuse that goes on in religious institutions and the difficulty in addressing them promptly. They must be addressed promptly and unequivocally, even if uncovered years later.

Because of my past, I think I have a different outlook on the role religion plays with a survivor of childhood abuse perpetrated by a leader in that religious community. Throughout the years there's no question I've had many internal discussions on the existence of God, including the one about if there was a God, how could he let something like this happen. I refuse to believe, as some do, that everything happens for a reason and ordeals are only placed on those who can handle them. I'm afraid that God, as one sees in the organized Church, didn't do a lot to help me through this, but God, as the one who exists in my spirit, brought a lot of comfort and strength during the most difficult times. I think some of the people in my extended family have the impression that unless you are a born again Christian and share that fellowship with other Christians, your faith cannot be real. Unfortunately, some also have the feeling that they are helping by trying to save your soul from eternal damnation.

A child abuse survivor can have very strong recollections, and even "flashbacks" of the assault. In the case of multiple assaults, it can last quite a long time because the one reminds them of the other and so on, and so on. It's little wonder that going inside a church can trigger intense traumatizing memories and that sense of danger can return.

With me, it wasn't so much the building that caused the flashbacks, but some of the memories that it brought back. I remember driving past the church building one day and seeing that it had been turned into a daycare centre of all things. I was able to process the thoughts that the physical building wasn't the cause of the assaults, but it certainly was significant in processing this part of my past.

Many of my Christian friends and some relatives are not aware of this part of my journey. There are those who don't see any harm in 'helping' by trying to expose me to the religion of my past, even though it wasn't a positive past for the most part. Through the years I've also felt that some of them deliberately exposed me to potentially traumatizing events to 'help' me past it.

One example, of course, is the family friend giving me the 'talk' about going on a date and not being used by a man who might just want one thing. If you remember, this was just before he forced me on the floor and tried to have sex with me.

Another example, although not nearly as damaging, is when someone close to our family gave me one page of sheet music of a song "In the Garden". This might seem trivial, but it was a song that a friend and I sang as a duet at church when we were kids. Both she and I went through some difficult times as kids. She was also a rebellious young woman, at least in the eyes of her father. My aunt in question is a deeply religious person, a nurse by profession, and would give much to those in need. But she is also a person who tends to think if you don't talk about it, it didn't happen, and people should be forgiven at all cost. Unfortunately, the person who needs forgiveness is the person who committed the crime, but the one who gets blamed is the person the crime was committed against.

In many cases, I felt I was getting blamed for not forgiving enough and daring to report and talk about the assault. My spirituality or Christianity had (and has) nothing to do with forgiveness because no matter what way you look at it, what happened was wrong and no amount of forgiveness was going to make it alright. Logically, I think my friends and family knew this, but there was sometimes a conniving way of convincing me I wasn't spiritually alright. I didn't go out and shout about my faith and attend church except on special occasions. To me, that was alright because my belief has always been that religion and spirituality should be something that guides and comforts you through life, not something that forces compliance from fear of going to hell. I am going to be a little sacrilegious here and admit that through the darkest parts of my journey, there were many times I felt I would be safer going to hell than spending eternity in heaven with my attackers.

I've often found that many organized religious communities have a perception of how a good Christian should act and anything other than that is not real Christianity. Similarly, when one is a preacher or leader in the religious community their job is to get you to conform to that perception for your own good. If you don't accept their 'help', it's you that has the problem and needs to be changed. I don't know how this can be when there is also an emphasis on freedom of choice and free will.

This fierce adherence to dogma was evident in my life in religion, politics, and everyday life. I don't think I or anyone else will ever understand it fully, but I think we have come further in realizing the impact the wars, crimes, and unkind practices of religious communities have on their victims. I don't think there will ever be anything worse than an organization that tries to cover up wrongdoing simply to protect their reputation at the expense of vulnerable victims of crimes against humanity, whether they're against one, hundreds, thousands, or millions of people. Many wars have been fought in the name of religion. Many crimes have been committed, and later covered up in order to protect the leadership of an organization at the expense of the victims.

I don't want you to think I don't value my spirituality because it has helped me through many difficult times. Partly because of my past, I don't accept an argument simply because of the role of the person promoting that argument. I tend to question and sometimes play the role of devil's advocate in an argument if I think the risk of accepting that argument is high. I look at all sides and make my decision based on the information. I think this is true in all areas of my life now, although I am also a strong believer in not taking a lot of risk and accepting experience of people who have been there. This too, was an issue for me sometimes, both in my mental health treatment and my religious encounters over the years. I came into a lot of situations where people didn't listen to what I was saying. Perhaps I wasn't saying it well. They would patronize me, tell me what I should be doing, what was wrong with me, and that I needed to get right with God before I'd be at peace. It was most often those people who were disturbing my peace.

PART THREE

BREAKING THROUGH THE TURMOIL AND OVERCOMING THE FEAR

This part of my narrative may seem strange to many because it focuses on some of the negative thought patterns initially. This was necessary for me, because it was only when I recognized these patterns that the healing could begin. What was very negative to me became the starting point of reframing my narrative. It allowed me to move past the feelings of intense fear, isolation, self-loathing, and anxiety.

BREAKING THROUGH – RECOGNIZING AN IMPORTANT THREAD!

∞

One of the most important moments in my breakthrough was recognizing what drove me as an individual and my philosophical outlook on life. Over the years, I've always been quite philosophical and the things I do have to have meaning for me. My mind has always worked in a philosophic and abstract, though usually logical, way in an effort to understand the meaning of life, so to speak. Post-traumatic stress took this to such an extreme that it was difficult for me to make sense of it. I couldn't have made any sense of it without professional psychological treatment.

I've often thought of things that make human beings human. Equally important, I've always tried to acknowledge what makes us unique as individuals. This was never more important than when I was trying to make sense of my past.

The big picture concept came into play a lot during the time I was experiencing an onslaught of post-traumatic stress symptoms. It was during this time that I felt worthless and that everything and everyone else was so much more important than I. I had to learn to narrow down my world view and put things into context to reframe the narrative of my life. Now that I've done much of that, I can see the concepts that have always had a big impact on my thoughts. Even in my world now, I try to focus on what's important to me and gives my life meaning.

When I moved from my hometown of Toronto after my first retirement, I worked in a policing organization as a civilian. Police organizations are very rank-oriented and depend on a chain of command for their operational functions, much like a paramilitary organization. In some ways, that makes sense. I've always had police and military people around me as family members so it's something I've always understood.

In my view, police are there to promote public safety for every citizen, regardless of background, religion, politics, beliefs, etc. Although there are many things the military and police could work on jointly, the distinction was, and is, extremely important. The military organization is there to protect our nation, our political infrastructure, and to follow the "Rules of Engagement" for military involvement. Their role is to protect our collective, whereas the police are there to protect us as individuals and ensure public safety.

This idea has been very important to me and has been a great source of comfort and pride as I recognize how much effort has been made to keep this distinction of roles between the police organization where I worked and the military. This has been evident when addressing challenges like First Nation protests where our political system has repeatedly failed an important segment of our country and our first people. It's been a great source of pride to me that the OPP has been vigilant in keeping public safety as their focus, rather than getting dragged into partisan politics.

During my university studies I learned that one of the most critical issues of Northern Ireland in the 1970's and 1980's was that the police force was often perceived to be an extension of the British Army. Public perception was often that police were more involved in maintaining the political structure in Northern Ireland than focusing on public safety. I've spent countless hours hoping that Canada never became another Northern Ireland in this way, and that we were able to maintain the distinctions needed between police and military.

When working with the OPP in later years, it became clear that there also needs to be a distinction between public safety and enforcement as everyone, regardless of their background and role in life, is entitled to public safety.

Concepts such as this had a huge impact on me throughout the years, in particular when I was being dragged kicking and screaming into situations that were more political in nature than simple business issues. It didn't surprise me at the bank when people played dirty politics because that's the way many people operated. Glazing over a situation and putting a spin on it was just something that was done. Part truths were a way of life and clear communication was something I never came to expect from anyone, although it would have made life so much easier.

My world was shattered when people I had worked with well in the past became a threat to me, which in turn made me feel isolated from everyone around me. The "cause" or "political goal" became the most important thing and people would go to any lengths to accomplish that goal or support their cause. I've always thought it's great and honourable to support a worthy cause, but there are limits on what should be done. It's also important for me to keep an open mind and not let a cause or goal prevent me from seeing the inherent risks or keep me from accepting change to save face. Anything worthwhile is worth fighting for. It's good to expand our mind to go to those uncomfortable places to discover the best way to support those goals or causes, but in a respectful way and always with integrity.

This was always in the back of my mind when contemplating life. It never came as a surprise when somebody supporting a cause, whether a political cause, a religion, or a charitable organization, was willing to reach their goal at the expense of somebody else.

Since childhood, I felt like others blamed me for the assaults against me or didn't believe me. Personally, I think people often avoid acknowledging traumatic events in order to maintain their beliefs and keep the faith in their church organization. Like conflict, we often ignore the situations, hoping they will go away. They don't usually go away but are left to fester and damage those directly involved and affected. At best, I felt that some people preferred to keep the dirty little secrets hidden. I often felt I would go to my grave without people knowing the truth because of rumours, lack of knowledge and covering up anything they felt would hinder their cause or make them feel uncomfortable.

It occurred to me they might look back every now and then, say "poor girl", then move on to the next thought without another backward glance. It also occurred to me they might attend my funeral, assuming I had one, reminisce about the good times, and again, never a backward glance. It would be as if I never existed, and all was in vain. Their goals would be realized at my expense and life would go on until the next victim came along. And all the time, it would be the victim's fault for not believing strongly enough, being in the wrong place at the wrong time, or just being in the way of a noble cause. This is still the way I feel at times, especially when working on social initiatives, and organizations who have to work hard to raise funds to do the work they do. I often feel that the people or organizations who offer the most funding are going to get better treatment, and acknowledged much more than those who aren't able to contribute financially as much.

"Putting a spin on things" became justification to do things that benefit themselves at the expense of others. "Branding" became a way to portray an organization in a way that they wanted others to see them even if wasn't reality. "Swishing" just took one swipe of the paint brush to cover up the sins of the past and create the picture you wanted others to see.

To me, that was so disturbing because my past had been manipulated by some who would take advantage of my vulnerability in order to gratify themselves, whether it was sexual gratification, financial gratification, or just a control thing where they wanted to exert pressure and show me who was boss. As soon as they accomplished their goal or saw me as a threat, they would throw me away like a piece of garbage and pretend nothing happened (or blame me if something did happen).

Another common thread was the concept of "good environment", both physical and psychological. This tormented me for a while because my mind was bringing the sins of my past into the forefront. It was reminding me that many people didn't know my past history and even if they did, so what? The church my parents and younger brother and sister attended for a while had the same name as a popular town in cottage country. I've never been to that town, but often thought I'd love to go because of the idyllic environment with parkland, wildlife, and fresh air. I had also seen advertising of a tower in that small town from which you could see for miles. Because of the connection my mind made with the church and that small town, I was horrified that people would think the church was idyllic and nothing bad could happen there. That church and that idyllic town, even though I had never been there, became the place where my mother's funeral was held, and a place where people covered up horrific crimes such as child molestation. This was my world for a while, with other people looking on and thinking how ideal everything was, while I sat there in isolation knowing that hell had happened in a church of the same denomination, and people were oblivious to the dangers that even they could face. This was one example where same names could be a psychological trigger for me.

This was just one more instance where something that is good and should make you feel peaceful, became something threatening and hostile. Worse than that, you were isolated and nobody would believe a word you said. The supposedly "good environment" was polluted and nobody knew the potential dangers, including me.

CHAPTER THIRTEEN

Starting Over Again

I DECIDED TO MOVE NORTH AND START OVER IN NEW SURROUNDINGS. I moved to a small city with a population of about 32,000. It was only an hour and a half from the places where my family in Ontario lived so it was still close enough to visit, yet far enough to feel like I was in different surroundings with two beautiful lakes close enough to walk to and relax in a peaceful atmosphere. I also had family about 45 minutes north who I could visit frequently. As it turned out, that was both a blessing and a curse, but mostly a blessing!

When I moved for my new start, I worked in the office of an insurance agent for just over a year. It was one of the worst jobs I ever had. It wasn't always the job itself, although that was pretty unpleasant. It was more the office environment, where everything was a joke and there was constant sexual innuendo.

The owner of the business, the insurance agent, made me feel like I was being quizzed on my past, whether it was my job at the bank, or more often my politics. I think the only reason he hired me was to use my financial services expertise in order to increase his portfolio of financial service clientele within his own business. That never materialized partly because I didn't show a lot of initiative in diving right into the insurance business. To me, it was even less scrupulous than the world of banking.

Before I moved, a cousin's spouse was a part owner of an insurance business but had since sold it. He tried to get me a job in that agency. I went to the interview but turned down the job. I wouldn't have been able to survive for a long time on the wage they had offered and was pretty sure I wouldn't like working there. My cousin's spouse was livid with me and the relationship went downhill. I felt bad but ultimately was glad I hadn't accepted the job. The agency would spend a lot of time and effort training me, only to have me quit. I hadn't felt that threatened in a long time.

As it turned out, a guy I went to high school with also worked there. He was one of the guys that Jane often belittled whenever we reminisced about our high school years. He had apparently asked her out when they were younger. She would laugh and say she was too beautiful and popular to be seen with a nerd like him. It's funny to realize what a small world it really is. The only reason I took the job at the insurance agency after I moved north was because I was now on my own again and had to pay my bills. I was quickly going through the money I had received when I left the bank and had to take a job to cover my expenses.

CHAPTER FOURTEEN

The Impact of the Past – Truth and Reconciliation

WHAT'S IMPORTANT TO ME

∞

T HE MOST IMPORTANT THING FOR MY HEALING WAS TO CONVINCE myself that my values, my beliefs, and what drove me as a person had not been wrong all these years. From a young age, I was forced to question people and things around me because of horrible circumstances that happened to me as a child. I was told to be silent at that time by some, and learned first-hand what an impact it can have on you and your whole family. As I got older and went to work for a living, one of the recurring things I faced was authority figures at work taking advantage of me in order to benefit themselves in one way or another. It's one thing to feel used when what you do benefits both, but when that benefit is only one-sided, it's not a good place to be.

At the same time, I was experiencing serious PTS symptoms, a major project was initiated at the bank. People who worked on it were sworn to secrecy and had to sign a non-disclosure agreement. I felt our job security was threatened if we dared question those in leadership. Those leaders were often unaware of the impact their decisions had on others, and quite honestly didn't care because that was just the cost of doing business.

The tension between business and technology was growing and there was a lot of mistrust. The "business" drove the budget and schedules which in turn, drove much of the quality of the initiatives. Unfortunately, the "technology" was at the mercy of their business partners and usually paid the price for the ignorance, lack of caring, unrealistic expectations and in some cases, disrespect that was the result of an unequal power struggle. Even when there was some care and respect shown to the partners in technology, the business partners were often unable, or unwilling, to speak up and cause a delay because of possible repercussions. To me, it was evident there was an unequal power struggle, and in most cases, the easiest thing for an area to do was to find somebody else to blame if things went wrong.

A BACKWARD GLANCE

To summarize how I explained to myself the many intrusive thoughts and PTSD symptoms I experienced, it was necessary to take a backward glance into my past. This was also how I was able to work through those thoughts and symptoms to some extent.

When I look back in time for a better understanding of this terrible journey, it makes more sense than I would have thought. The scrambled folders of past experience were out of whack but they did make some sense. One of the most horrifying parts of my journey centred around world history and the absolute terror that something as horrible as the holocaust was going to happen right here in Canada. My past includes a Romanian grandfather who was interred in Kapuskasing after he immigrated to Canada; an Irish grandmother whose family was discriminated against because of their Irish Catholic background; a grandfather from a well-off Newfoundland family who was disowned because he married a Nova Scotian woman from a working-class family.

My more recent history included extended family with religious disharmony stemming partly from the troubles in Northern Ireland; childhood sexual abuse; and being uprooted several times; partly because of this past. It includes an extended family whose actions and words minimized this horrendous personal past, and in some cases, blamed the victim for not "getting over it" (partly because I didn't share the same vigour in expounding a religion). I was always a child who liked to get along with people, picked my battles, and questioned something before I acted on it.

My personal history included philosophical, political, and historical teachings that increased my knowledge of history and the survival of horrible events, such as the holocaust, civil war, and terrorism. My education included reading Victor Frankl, R.D. Laing, and others who tried to make sense of surviving tragedy and dealing with the politics of human interactions.

My recent history included an increased awareness of groups such as the paramilitary groups in Northern Ireland and the Romanian Iron Guard. It included stories from friends of different backgrounds and classes and memories of discrimination, both personal and stories from friends. I tried to find out more about my Romanian grandfather. My horror came from thinking he could have come from a past that saw him leave his homeland because of family involvement in horrific war crimes, or just as likely, fleeing a homeland that saw him fighting for his life because of Jewish pogroms that would have been a reality at that time. Either way, my present at that time was one of utter confusion, horrible intrusive memories and being frozen in a very unkind past. I still have questions that I will never be able to answer. But it isn't as disturbing to me now because it is just memories, not a constant barrage of terror.

IMPACTS - NEWS, CORNWALL INQUIRY, VOLUNTEER WORK

∞

After I left, or was let go from the insurance company, I volunteered with the local police detachment and started working part-time in the community service office. The only good thing that came out of the insurance company is that I became familiar with the local police detachment through the insurance company's safety program that taught children to stay away from unfamiliar dogs. From that, I started to volunteer and became heavily involved with community safety initiatives, both in my paid employment with the police service and my volunteer work.

It was a stressful job insofar as I didn't have an outlet. I never felt like I could express my frustrations even though others could. I often felt my opinion didn't matter. The combination of part-time work and what turned out to be a full-time volunteer role consumed my waking hours. This paid job and the volunteer work were often closely related, with the same people out of the same office. I felt I was often taken advantage of but didn't always express my opinion or complain because public and community safety initiatives were that important to me.

My driving force was that I didn't want others to go through the same experiences that I did, especially as a child and young woman. My goal was to focus on prevention rather than enforcement because I was determined that people should not have to go through such trauma in the first place. Enforcement should happen when it does, but the best option was to prevent crimes, especially violent crimes, from happening.

Part of the job sometimes reminded me of my Post-Traumatic Stress symptoms, such as when I was reading the media reports in the Canadian news about a prominent Inquiry, called the Cornwall Inquiry. One of the objectives of the Cornwall Inquiry was to determine if victims of sexual assault should be publicly named, even without their consent. My level of stress increased substantially waiting for the court's decision. To me, it would have been like handing a loaded firearm to someone to use against me as a victim of sexual crimes. I was obviously relieved when the court came to what I felt was the right decision, to protect the identity of sexual assault victims so they're not revictimized.

Another thing the Cornwall Inquiry caused me to ponder was whether we should even report assault or not. Even though this sounds like a ludicrous question, it is one that really needs to be taken into consideration when we're talking about childhood abuse and sexual assault. Ideally, it's best to report the crimes, obviously, because we don't want them to happen to another person. But there's a very real feeling of danger when you do report them. Whether we like to admit it or not in this progressive age in which we live, there is still a very real stigma that goes along with being a rape victim, especially in our legal system. It's the defense attorney's job to discredit the victim and make it seem like it was a consensual act if possible. Often in the case of a violent attack, our memory can be fuzzy for a while and we might not recall exactly what happened to us until later when we've been able to process the event. My biggest issue was with sequence of events and the order in which they occurred. I think this is because there were multiple assaults in my past, and the horrible memories that caused the intense fear and feeling of possible death became blurred as a single big event until I was able to pull them apart and "refile" the information in the appropriate folders of my memory.

I always thought it best to report crime, but was sympathetic to anyone who didn't, or couldn't. I think my experience as a child affected me later on when I was assaulted, because I wasn't aware of the consequences to the first perpetrator until my mid-thirties. Even then, it was not much of an impact on me because he only got a sentence of 6 months psychiatric treatment for what he did to me. He picked up his career afterwards and there didn't seem to be any repercussions for him, other than any guilt he may have felt; meanwhile there were certainly serious consequences for me.

When I was assaulted as a young adult, there was an added fear that my family would be torn apart again since the perpetrator was the "good one". There was a very real possibility that I would not be believed. There was an added fear that I would be blamed; after all he was a pillar of the community, and I was a young adult who should be able to look after myself. At that time, what he did was not considered a crime because there was no penetration. I would have been reporting it for no other reason than destroying my family and causing myself to go through a horrendous legal process once again, and for what!

When a later acquaintance assaulted me, I think the memory got pushed to the back of my mind very quickly. I truly believe that I would not have been able to report it at the time. I also convinced myself that I was the stupid one for asking him for the ride home. Again, there was the guilt and a very real situation of self-blame. In that situation, he was a very popular, well-respected pillar of the community and it would be me that got the worst of any legal encounter. Later when this became part of my Post-Traumatic Stress Disorder symptoms, it became a real threat to my life and my sanity. My third assaulter was part of a well-known community group and an Irish folk band.

In Canada, the violent conflict in the Irish community was something that wasn't apparent. Some of the people I knew and came to know emigrated to Canada to remove themselves from the violence in Northern Ireland and escape the terror that existed in both extreme factions. This was one of the many prejudices against Catholics in Northern Ireland. It's this part of the history that created tension between my Protestant relatives and my education that makes me lean towards the Catholic and more left-wing Irish politics. Most of the traditional media and textbooks of Irish history leaned towards the Ulster Protestant version of colonial history and characterized Catholics as "terrorists" and pro IRA. Many were not, and most were not violent. Both Catholic and Protestant sides of the conflict had violent extremist factions.

In Irish politics, it was often the case when referring to an organization such as the Irish Republic Army, that there would be a "splinter" group when more violent members felt they were becoming too "status quo". During my lifetime this occurred several times, first when the more violent group, the Provisional IRA came into being because the original IRA was more willing to negotiate and come to political solutions. After a while, the Provos became less violent and the "Real IRA" was formed to keep using extreme violence in their fight. Both were considered "splinter groups". I had never discussed politics with my attacker and have no idea what his thoughts towards extremism and terrorism are, but the thought that he would know someone who was capable of killing me was very possible, and to some extent, the thought still crosses my mind every now and then. He was a head-hunter in the corporate world and very well connected in the community so there was no doubt in my mind that he would be believed and I would not.

I reported the third sexual assault many years later to the police service where it occurred. I didn't expect anything would ever come of it, but still reported the assault and hoped to get some closure, whatever that is. Years before, I felt I was at fault and would have paid an unbearable price for tarnishing the name of a pillar of the community. When I reported it, I was also volunteering for Victim Services. I felt I couldn't support victims of sexual assault if I was feeling guilty for not reporting a crime, even though it was many years ago. I couldn't remember all the details, such as the date it happened, but I remembered many of the details of the actual assault. This was a part of my history that violently flashed back to me as if it had been yesterday. Sometimes in the decade before my reporting of the crime, I had felt like it was happening to me all over again, even to the point of the physical pain in my lower back, and his hand violently holding my mouth shut.

CHAPTER FIFTEEN

Full circle. Finding my spirit

NOTHING WAS MORE IMPORTANT TO ME THAN THESE TWO THINGS: regaining my memory and the ability to live life without looking over my shoulder every minute of every day.

Over the years, I have been able to recognize when others, especially family members, had clouded judgement of my reality and tried to impose their beliefs on what happened to me in the past. I recognized they had the right to forgive, but only on their behalf, not mine. The friends and family members who were most religious, other than my father and a few friends, were the ones most likely to blame me for my difficulties.

One person was even willing to look past the criminals and violent people in my background to move forward herself. That in itself was her choice, but she also tried to impose it on me. Initially I felt she was a great support and was looking out for my well-being. That soon changed and I felt that her judgement was harming my ability to move past the hurt. She had been a nurse, and often felt that her experience in the profession was still current and unquestionable. She was an expert at distancing herself from the wrongs and was very capable of manipulating a situation to her liking. A few times, I felt that I was a character in the movie, *One Flew Over the Cuckoo's Nest*, and she was my Nurse Ratchett. That was probably the thing that scared me most, because with people like that looking out for me, I was doomed to be consumed by mistakes of the past and never regain a voice for myself.

The thing that disturbed me most was her faith and ability to overlook evils of the world in hope of a better place and redemption. She saw the world through rose-coloured glasses and imposed this distorted version of reality on those around her. I'm sure she never meant any harm by it, but it doesn't help one trying to recover from psychological trauma. I can understand the need to gloss over some past hurts, but the people who should get the most compassion are the innocent victims, not the perpetrators, and in her case, I often felt she had more compassion for the perpetrators if they were religious people.

I recall a thought pattern that I had frequently. If only I could wait until the afterlife, everything would be alright. I for one, don't want to wait until the afterlife, and certainly don't want to get there sooner because of somebody's inability to face a difficult reality. That was an important issue to address in my recovery: I needed to overcome the fear that someone close to me was willing to see me lose my happiness, and even my safety, in order to strengthen their religious beliefs and their inability to see the world for what it sometimes was.

Spirituality was the part of my human spirit that was most badly damaged. I discovered that I had to let my spirit free itself from all past hurts and become connected to myself again, not a separate entity out there somewhere. I had to recognize that I may never live up to the expectations of some of my extended family. I was at peace with that. I had to realize that they were not better than me simply because they went to church every week. I had to realize that I couldn't look down on them simply because they did.

It was difficult convincing myself that my thoughts on the matter were important and my beliefs and way of living was just as valid as theirs. To force myself into their way of thinking would harm an integral part of me and move me backwards into the past. My experience with Post-Traumatic Stress made me think of religion in a whole different light, and in extreme cases, reminded me of a cult where people lose the ability to think for themselves. My spirituality became a very independent part of me, and I was finally able to balance that part of my human spirit that had been so seriously damaged by past experiences.

Probably the second most important thing to me was for someone to listen and not judge me. One of the most damaging things to go through when you've been abused or sexually assaulted is the fact that people judge you and think you're not telling the truth. This stems back to my childhood when the important people in my life did believe me. But a key part of my support system at that time, namely the church, tried to cover it up. I think they believed me but were willing to cover up the crime to protect the reputation of their organization. This past wound made judgement-free listening so critical to me in the modern day.

The ability to tell my story is still a recurring effort and probably the one that impacts me the most. There have been times when people have wanted me to tell my story but didn't want to hear it. When this happens, I go back to the times I was silenced. In extreme cases, when I was suffering most from flashbacks, this would take me back to a very vivid memory of someone holding their hand over my mouth and ramming themselves into me. A faded memory of a harsh reality that allowed me to survive in the past was now very present and real. I remember throughout my recovery that the thing I thought would be the deadliest "trigger" would be to have a hand placed over my mouth to force silence. I often saw that hand coming towards me and it scared me.

I've often been in positions where privacy and confidentiality were critical and I take this very seriously. At the height of my experience with Post-Traumatic Stress, I felt I couldn't say anything to anybody. I was in complete isolation from everyone around me. My biggest fear was saying the wrong thing and having people misinterpret me and thinking I was that horrible person again who reported it. It seemed that everyone else could say anything, but if I did, the sky would fall and there would be major repercussions. At the time, silence was my only option and it was killing me. It took a huge effort on my part to be able to trust anyone again. I don't know that I will ever trust most people completely again, but I hope someday I will be able to take that step toward recovery.

Another important change was to allow myself to relax and not always think about work. Work had become the only thing that made me feel like I was worth anything, especially when my home life with Joe became too much to cope with. My horrible experiences at the bank seriously damaged any feeling of self-worth. Everything I had previously accomplished seemed meaningless. I'd wasted my entire life working at a job that gave me little satisfaction. It took me the longest time to realize I was very good at my job, treated people with respect, and accomplished a lot, sometimes in spite of my surroundings.

Unfortunately, I also felt that this was my downfall, but I'd have it no other way. At least my conscience didn't keep me awake at night. I still have issues with this sometimes because I feel my life hasn't had much of an impact on the world. I've lost contact with most people from my past. I've pulled away from those who didn't respect my situation. I have no desire to relive the past. I find many past acquaintances, especially extended relatives, only want to reminisce about the wonderful past we had. Mine wasn't great and I have no desire to pretend it was.

That being said, I am capable of appreciating the positive effect many of my family, friends and experiences have had on my life. I've learned to give them full credit when it's due, but also to recognize when I'm being pulled backwards in time to an uncomfortable place. The only person who should be able to take me back to that uncomfortable place is me, and I can assure you that writing this book is doing that very well. Sometimes I like to reminisce to remind myself and family and friends of the good times we had together. But I am now able to determine when others want to reminisce only to convince me that some family members and experiences really weren't that bad. I think they'd probably think differently if they were more directly affected.

When the two later assaults happened, it was only me that I could blame for not reporting it. I felt I had been through enough already and knew what the outcome would be. Nobody would believe me. It would be my fault that it happened, and I would have been the girl who tried to ruin the reputation of well-connected men. In the latter case, I also blamed myself because I had asked him for the ride home. In that situation I silenced myself, but it was out of true fear and uncertainty at the time.

An important accomplishment was learning to forgive myself and allow myself to move forward and place blame on others, if and when it was appropriate. This was particularly true in the attempted assault and sexual assault when I was older. I always blamed myself for not acting sooner or more forcefully when under attack. In both cases, it took a long time before I could place the blame on my assaulters. I was the victim in both cases regardless of their stature in the community and their ability to rationalize what they had done. I was not to blame, and realizing this was an important step for me.

I found that forgiving myself, and to some extent, the perpetrators, allowed me to move forward. I have come to terms that neither will ever be held accountable on this earth for what they did. I don't dwell on that, and it doesn't impact me as much anymore. I am able to move forward and put both of these horrible experiences as historical markers of my past, and only a memory. I recognize they have had an effect on me, but they don't make me who I am today. I still deal with these events insofar as I'm not really free to speak of them without consequences. If I were now to speak about the one assault, my family would be hurt and, in some cases probably outraged that I would accuse him of such a thing. I know there will never be consequences for him, partly because at the time what he did was not illegal. I did report the sexual assault by the acquaintance but doubt there will ever be a consequence for him. He, too, was a pillar of the community and it's a situation where it would be my word against his. I do still have some fear in this case. I know that if someone is willing to force themselves on someone, they probably wouldn't hesitate to do further damage if they felt threatened.

All this being said, I have moved forward and feel relatively safe from those two events of my past. The biggest impact on me now is that I don't want to go on pretending nothing happened when faced with get-togethers and events where I might run into one of the perpetrators. I also don't want to partake in conversations that hold him in an esteemed position. When I say that, I'm not being angry or hurt, but have come to the conclusion that I can't deny the wrongs of my past anymore and pretend everything was alright. It most certainly was not!

Another impact of these incidents is that I don't have a lot of contact with some friends and relatives anymore. I miss the camaraderie we once had as young people. I don't blame this all on what happened; a big part of it is life itself. Families grow apart as they marry into other families and have families of their own. I never did that, so I became more isolated. I think I've also been affected by responses over the years that minimized my feelings and manipulated the situation to fit in with their ideals and beliefs. I used to be much closer to my extended family, but now find it difficult to pretend that the past was good more than it was bad.

SECONDARY TRAUMA – BROUGHT ME TO MY KNEES

Many of us have heard of secondary trauma, most often in reference to people who witness horrible events in their line of work. This would include military personnel, police officers, paramedics, firefighters, many health professionals, 911 operators, and more. I can say firsthand that this is very real. It's serious and can be as debilitating as those who develop PTSD as a victim of a horrible event. My belief is most people enter these professions out of empathy and their desire to help others, keeping in mind that everyone needs to make a living as well. It's about time we've started to realize the impact that facing trauma every day has on us. It can take its toll on people.

I found in my own life that secondary trauma brought me to my knees more than once and I was frozen in time so much that I couldn't make a decision. As I was going through the worst of my nightmare, I sometimes stayed away from the news and newspapers because I knew they would trigger past memories. I couldn't help but see the headlines on the front page if I was out. They sometimes triggered horrible memories. One example of this was seeing the headline that several people in Quebec had been killed in a bus accident. I cried because I was pretty sure it was Joe's parents who were killed, although they hadn't gone back to Quebec for years and were nowhere near the accident. It was just my mind connecting events that were in no way connected.

When I saw the news and there was tragedy and horror, I would relate too much to it and it caused me to sink further into isolation. I started seeing more about Post-Traumatic Stress Disorder and thinking that must be what I was dealing with. I often thought that was what I had but would fight it because I was never in a combat situation. My own war was here at home in the peaceful country of Canada. My own ignorance told me that only military people who were in the midst of a war could have PTSD. I fought it because I refused to think I was at war with my past. I now think the symptoms are the same but the content of the flashbacks is different.

As I recovered, one of the things I noticed more was the pain of other people and thinking their pain was much worse than my own. Who was I to think I should feel bad about what happened to me, when there were other people worse off than I? It took me the longest time to convince myself that I was worth taking care of.

Another of the darkest parts of my journey took me back to my history lessons and stories about World War II when the Jews were slaughtered by Hitler's army simply because of who they were. For some reason, I had intrusive thoughts of the Holocaust happening all over again, not necessarily with only Jewish people being targeted, but anyone who was vulnerable and unable to fend for themselves. In retrospect, we know that genocides have happened since then and we haven't overcome the bigotry and hatred that allows human beings to perpetrate such horrors against each other. My mind was often racing during my waking hours and horrific historical events were usually a part of the barrage of information that consumed my thoughts. I was fearful that such an atrocity would happen again.

A big issue with these thought patterns was the absolute terror that they caused. It was now bigger than just me and the persons who assaulted me. It was now something that could possibly harm a lot of people, all in the name of a "cause". I was frozen in time; a time in the past where nobody was safe, including me, my family and friends. I was never a fan of martyrdom and felt nobody should have to pay the ultimate sacrifice, especially in a war they never chose to join.

Post-Traumatic Stress Disorder is just that; a war. Unfortunately, those affected by it never had that choice, and it's something that will affect them for the rest of their life. There is the possibility they will be able to recover and lead a reasonably normal life, whatever that may be, but that experience changes you forever. The one thing we can do is provide more support for those going into a profession where the risk of PTSD is higher than most. We owe it to those who risk their lives every day to make our world a safer place.

Post-Traumatic Stress Disorder is an experience I wouldn't wish on my worst enemy. I will confess there were brief moments when I wished someone inflicting a lot of psychological pain on me could understand what they were putting me through. Yes, there were some who I think intentionally tried to make me focus on things I had worked so hard to forget in the years after I experienced them. I will never understand how anyone can be so brutal in the way they treat a person. I've gotten past most of these feelings and prefer to chalk it up to stupidity and ignorance, rather than malice. I sometimes think I might be too generous in thinking that, but it helps me cope.

TURMOIL AS PART OF MY HEALING JOURNEY

∞

It might seem strange that I consider this part of my healing journey. At the time, these horrible memories brought me to a point in my life when I didn't know if I would survive all of the turmoil. In retrospect, this also helped me recognize that something was happening in my mind that wasn't entirely based on my present circumstances and reality. It was the intrusion of some memories, such as news events, that helped me realize I was somewhere between fact, past and present reality at the time. It also made it extremely difficult to make a decision and move forward. It was exhausting to make the distinction between my own experiences, those of others, news stories and what had happened in the past as opposed to what was happening in the present.

Sometimes the response was simply to "tune out" and freeze because the fear of making a wrong decision and causing someone else to get hurt was so great. I think, at this stage, I wasn't too concerned if something happened to me, but I was always in great fear that someone else would be hurt because of me. One of the most difficult things for me, was to distinguish my present reality from my past reality. It was often this turmoil that helped me make that distinction. As difficult as it was, this was part of my healing journey.

I wish I had written more of this turmoil down at the time because it would have helped me write these memoirs more effectively. One of the things that always concerned me was privacy. I think this is partly due to the gossip that surrounded my childhood abuse at a time when victim blaming was even worse than it is now. I always had it in the back of my mind that someone would find what I was writing and it would reflect badly on my family who has always been my main support, especially through the difficult times.

This also played into my fear that some people from my past have caused me horrendous pain, and for some reason always come out smelling like roses. Several examples of this are Jane and of course my assaulters. Jane and a perpetrator caused me great pain because they knew of the past childhood assault and used that information to reduce me to a pile of rubble trying to survive. Throughout my healing journey I never wished any harm to come to either one of them, but I was also terrified that they would be seen as my saviour for disclosing my past to others, especially in the case of Jane. This often put the image in my head of the fireman who set the place on fire and then received accolades for extinguishing it. The fire shouldn't have been set in the first place. This probably was, and in some cases, still is the thing that holds me back from going all out and reaching out to others. I hope my journey eventually takes me to a place where I won't feel like this anymore.

The turmoil through some of my personal relationships was not the only difficult part of my healing journey. As I mentioned, I exposed myself to things I knew would be painful. An example of this is TV shows that had to do with sexual assault and violence. I was so sensitive at the time that I knew if I could watch them without breaking down, I would be able to get through the day. I now know that exposure therapy is something that is used for people with PTSD. I often wonder about it. I am concerned that if it's the therapy of choice and somebody isn't ready to go into those dark periods of their past, it could be deadly. One regret I do have is not going to a qualified therapist sooner to help me get through that dark part of my journey with a little less pain than I experienced.

It has also been a difficult part of my healing journey to write these memoirs to some extent. Allowing anyone to read the narrative about my past was paralyzing at times. I've worried about my privacy, more importantly my immediate family's privacy, and often shut myself down to protect them from the gossip that was almost my demise. I know, in some regards, this fear shouldn't have as big of an impact on me as it does any more. That being said, it's hard to change your personality. All these years, I've been a fairly reserved individual who doesn't like to hear gossip or make light of other people's issues.

Throughout this journey, I haven't been asked by most friends, or former friends, how they could have been more supportive. For some reason people have felt it was alright to 'help' me without my consent. I often felt that people from my past tried to highlight all of the good experiences they had, knowing full well that my experiences were horrendous during the same timeframes. It questioned my integrity and made me feel that I shouldn't feel the way I felt. It minimized the horrible experiences I had endured, and was similar to someone just yelling out, "Get over it." When somebody manipulates, misrepresents, or simply acts without knowing the truth to 'help' you, it often makes matters worse. One of the nicest things someone can do to support you through a difficult time is simply to be there in case you want to talk and recognize that only you can solve your issues with the necessary supports and make things right again.

The worst example of someone else taking control of my life is that of Jane. I had no idea she was circulating the news of my history to others, including the person who I eventually had a close relationship with, Joe. She told him of the childhood assaults, the later assault, and misrepresented to him that my third attacker was a former boyfriend. When I finally asked her about it, she said she had no idea the two of us would end up together. She also claimed she told him to 'help' me, and ensure he would be nicer to me. Neither made any sense to me at all. Telling someone intimate details of your past is not helpful, unless, of course, it's to report a crime or literally save a life. Instead, what Jane did was hand the weapon to someone who would eventually use that information to destroy me and cause illness and injury. Not helpful.

If she had asked me if she could share that information with people I work with, I would have said no, don't. There was absolutely no reason for her to do that. My story was my story to tell if and when I chose to share those details.

Trying to take the steering wheel of your own life away from you is counterproductive and often damaging. My journey has made me realize a balance is required between telling my story and letting the past be the past. That balance has been difficult to find and will always be a challenge that I have to face head on.

PERSON: HEALING YOURSELF WITH SUPPORT

∞

Recovery – how do I recover from something like my past? I thought it would be much easier to figure out how I could get through this and recover, but it wasn't. One of the healers of PTSD is time, coupled with therapy. It took a long time before I even recognized my previous self. I was once a calm, cool, collected person who could tackle difficult projects without getting rattled.

This was my perception of myself when I entered the working world in my early twenties. I could take on almost any challenge my various jobs had to offer. The childhood abuse, bank robberies and violent scenarios were something I thought I handled reasonably well with calmness. I didn't let them rattle me, or so I thought.

When the PTSD symptoms started affecting me more, I became an anxiety-filled person who found it difficult to be around people, difficult to be alone, and panicked anytime I thought something bad would happen. I still appeared calm, cool, and collected to most people, but inside there was turmoil. I no longer thought of myself that way. It took me more than two years after leaving the bank to feel less anxious. During those two years I was isolated.

I took courses to feel productive and to try and help me focus more. My mind was constantly racing at that time and I thought taking courses would let me concentrate better. It did. That being said, I'm glad it was distance education because it gave me the opportunity to read, reread, and reread again until the information sank in. I think, if I had been listening to lectures at that time, most of the information would have gone in one ear and out the other because of the constant racing of my mind.

PTSD can make it difficult to concentrate and retain information. Rereading course material was necessary. It was also nice that some of the courses I took reminded me of my first years at university and brought back much of the information I had learned during those earlier years. Going back to university decades later gave me a more expanded context and perception. After all, I had lived decades of my own life experiences by that time.

I also listened to a lot of music and did a little writing. I would go for walks in the daytime but that was the furthest I would go. I did go out for social events a few times, but rarely. I also took a few journeys into my past to help me remember events and places that I was fuzzy about. I don't know if that was a good thing to do, but it seemed to help me refocus my memory and regain confidence that my past was in fact real. It was difficult.

I got professional help to ground me and put things in perspective. Advice I've tried to follow is if you can't control what's happening, learn how to respond to it well. When I read my own writing about my past, it became clearer that one of the ways I got through the PTSD symptoms was to recognize that I had little or no control over it. When I refer to myself in this context, I also include my family because they are an important part of me. I couldn't control the memories, but I did have some control over my responses, including the fear. It's tough, but it can be done.

Some of the journey was 'going with the flow', through the bad times, knowing, or at least hoping, that I would come out of it at the other end, probably with some damage, but at least alive. When I look back now, I am amazed I survived this part of my recovery. It's quite remarkable that I survived my recovery from 1997 onward because when I remember that time now, there were a lot of overwhelming situations that could have been the end of me, both figuratively and literally.

It makes more sense to me now that I know more about PTSD and some of the therapies that are used to treat people with this injury. These include Exposure Therapy, EMDR (Eye Movement Desensitisation Reprocessing), and talk therapy. Some of my treatment involved going back to the traumas and beginning to "reprocess" those memories so I didn't remain stuck in that loop.

PTSD causes this "remembering" in such a way that you're there again, feeling the same intensity, the same emotion and even some of the physical pain. My layperson description of this is that you've shoved these memories and emotions way back in your mind because they're too painful to process. At the most inopportune time, they decide to rear their ugly heads and force you to reprocess them. You weren't able to process them the first time around, so it's not surprising you can't process them any better now.

In fact, in my case it was worse the second, third, and fourth time around because every other event that reminded me of these traumas reappeared at the same time. It's important to get professional help to remember and reprocess the traumas in such a way that they don't overwhelm and terrify you all over again. One of the things I read that made sense to me is that you have to create your narrative, or your story of that event so you're able to move past it. Every story has an opening, a body, and a closing. You have to create the narrative that allows you to write the closing of that trauma story.

Once I felt I was up for it, I started doing things I knew would make me face my worst fears. One of the things I did was to expose myself to television shows that I knew would remind me of the assaults. The one I watched the most was *Law & Order: Special Victims Unit*, mainly because it dealt with sexual assault in almost every episode, but it was not extremely graphic. I felt if I could watch that, I could deal with anything that might trigger my past memories. It did, but there were certainly some tears along the way.

Another thing I did to get rid of the flash backs, was to go out west and meet the man who assaulted me when I was a child. Part of it was to get his side of the story, and part of it was to see if I had moved past it and forgiven enough to get rid of the angst and anger. A large part of it was also to regain my memory and to see if I remembered what he looked like or if I was imagining what I thought he looked like. It made me feel better when I recognized him as soon as I saw him. It helped me realize I was not making up a certain image, and it allowed me to put to rest the thought that everyone I saw could be him.

I'll talk about a few things that helped me in more detail. They focused on both the good and the bad things I experienced, but that were necessary for me to find balance. I think I mentioned before that I have always been an optimist. One of the bad things about being an optimist is that you always see the good in people, but sometimes don't take the bad as seriously as you should. You have an "it can only get better" attitude when in reality, it will only get better if you do something to change things and make that happen. The most important thing for me to find was that balance where I could put things into the past again where they belonged, and also put them into perspective. It's difficult to do this after the past has reared its ugly head again and becomes an all-consuming part of your present once again. But it can be done. It must be done!

One of my main "daymares" was with some initiatives focusing on cultural change in many organizations today. With initiatives focusing on changing the culture of an organization, they often "demand" we only focus on the positive and ignore some of the resistance and risk they will face. It reminded me that many were willing to take big risks because they felt the "ends justified the means." I don't believe this is true and feel that how we get there is just as important as the goals we want to achieve.

This is part of that "It can only get better" attitude. It's vital that we focus on both the positive and negative if we want to affect change. We also have to recognize that what is positive for one person might be negative for another. We have to determine what we want to accomplish and recognize there are different ways to reach that goal. History tells us both things that worked well and what didn't work well.

I certainly understand that we tend to go first to the negative feelings when we suffer with PTSD. It's called "self-preservation". With PTSD, the symptoms are also based on something very real that happened. But we need to know this if we want to avoid the same mistakes over and over again. I've often thought the choices we can make in response to anything is limited and we, as humans, tend to choose what we think would be the easiest. Well, the easiest isn't always the best.

FINDING MY VOICE AGAIN

∞

Something that affected me deeply was that I felt I could no longer talk to anyone about anything. I felt the rumours and gossip about my past and recent present being passed around mercilessly at my workplace and some of it was untrue. Worse than that, I felt I was considered weak because I let it happen.

Pity and a "poor thing" mentality are not helpful when you've been a strong and resourceful person up until that time. I didn't need to be "looked after" if that's what people thought they were doing at the time. I needed to have support in the work I was doing just like every other person I worked with. That support was not there, in fact, just the opposite. I was either being avoided like the plague or used by several who saw the opportunity to condescend and humiliate me.

It was urgent for me to feel comfortable enough to speak to people again and not feel attacked or misunderstood. It was also important for me to clarify some of the "untruths" that I felt were being spread around about me.

I was absolutely petrified to talk in case anyone took my words out of context or gave them a different meaning from what was intended. As a result, I withdrew and found it difficult to talk to anyone. One day I saw a poster on the wall at work. It was for a speech club. I read more about it and decided to join. I felt this was the safest place for me to relearn speaking to people and learning to trust again. It did help. I stepped way out of my comfort zone and wrote a few speeches about my past without giving too much detail, but I think enough to clarify some of the untruths. It was also my way of telling my own story instead of someone else telling it with the misconceptions, their spin, and the untruths that were very damaging to me. Most of these speeches were received well, and most importantly, with respect. Respect was something that I felt was completely taken away from me at that time and it was important that I regained at least some of it. For me, this club was that place.

THE PHYSICAL TOLL OF PTSD

∞

PTSD also takes a toll on your physical well-being. I've had back problems since my mid 20's, but they were more bothersome than debilitating. I found when the PTSD symptoms got worse, so did my back problems. When I was assaulted by my third attacker, it was my back that took the brunt of the pressure during the assault. I still find when I'm stressed out, my lower back stiffens up and aches.

Another physical reaction I had to stress was stomach problems. Gravol was a dear friend for a very long time. The way I coped with facing a difficult activity, such as reporting a crime, was to take a heavy plastic bag with me. This gave me a sense of security, and allayed my fear that I would throw up all over someone or something. I think that was one of my strongest fears, even more than the event itself that prevented me from facing some of the things that made me uncomfortable.

I also recall when stress brought on fainting spells, and at times, an asthma attack. This happened more when I was younger, but also as an adult a few times.

I often didn't realize what was happening and had medical tests more than once to rule out serious illnesses. My medical doctors were also at a loss sometimes to explain why I was fainting. I still watch my health and carry a puffer in case of an asthma attack, but I rarely have to use it anymore.

I still find my back and muscles tensing when my level of stress rises, but I am much better at recognizing that now and can ease the pain and discomfort by focusing on my breathing, taking a walk, doing some yoga, or meditating.

WALKING

A good walk always allowed me to clear my mind and focus on things around me. This was also difficult at times because you have to put yourself outside of your comfort zone and be in open places.

It also allowed me to "write" in my head and clear some of the confusion. Often when I wanted to write I could go for a walk and clarify my thoughts before heading home and putting some of the words on paper.

There is also something to be said for getting out in nature. Letting nature ground and inspire you, feeling its healing energy can be a great way to change your perspective and find balance when everything seems too much to handle.

For me, nature brought peace and comfort in a very holistic way. It made me realize I was a small part of a vast world, and an important, appreciative part who could make a difference. I could breathe in the air around me and find peace. I felt small, yet relaxed and one with my surroundings. When the earth was quiet around me, nothing could cause me pain.

JOURNALING

∞

I also took up journaling, initially every day. This was suggested to me by a therapist and it's one of the things that helped me through the tough times once I could make sense of it again. She requested that I made a point to write at least a few things a day that were positive. Initially this was tough. I did this even on those days when it felt next to impossible; even if it was something as small as a flower blooming, or sunshine. It had to be anything that would cause the raging memories to stop so I could see something positive. Being an optimistic and positive person, this was one of the biggest challenges for me. My personality characteristics always took me to positive thoughts first. The PTS symptoms rewired my mind to go to the things that terrified me first. It took me years to re-learn my dominant personality characteristics and to manage it so I could focus on the positive thoughts first again.

Tied to noticing and writing down the positive is the gift of gratitude. Even in our darkest times, gifts abound if we're open to see them. We sometimes don't allow ourselves to recognize these gifts and we often forget to appreciate them. As you turn your focus to the positive, taking a moment to think of something you're grateful for (no matter how simple) can help reclaim solid ground.

Journaling was also something that helped me remember some of my dreams and nightmares. I've never been one who could remember dreams after I woke up. The only exception to this was one nightmare from my childhood that stayed with me. It was after watching a tv show with one of my older brothers. There must have been a giant spider in that episode because I woke up screaming thinking there was a giant spider in my bed. To this day, I don't like spiders. My older brothers and I got along well, and still do. This is one time my second oldest brother wasn't too impressed with his kid sister because he wasn't allowed to watch that show again when I was around.

When I woke up after a dream, I would make a point to write it down as much as I could. I never really got the knack of writing down nightmares, though I do remember a combination of nightmare and dream once my thought processes started to settle down.

Journaling gave me an opportunity to go back and read how I was feeling at the time and how far I had come in my healing journey. I made a point not to go back and read them a lot, but every now and then I would refresh my memory of the turmoil. I didn't go back to them a lot while writing this memoir either but there are some events, memories, thought processes, and feelings that are recorded in both.

At one point, I also started another journal because I found it too difficult to put both positive and negative in the same book. At the time, I was trying too hard to get the negative thoughts out of my brain, and it didn't make sense to intersperse it with the positive. I found myself always focusing on the negative.

Writing actually helps you get things out of your system, much like talking to a professional. It helps you make sense of things and create that all important narrative that helps you process thoughts. The second journal was my "positive journal" and it forced me to write positive and uplifting thoughts again. It also gave me a safe and positive place to read about my thoughts when I was feeling down. My other journal was something I avoided reading because it would only remind me of this big mess called my life.

PATTERNS I NOTICED ALONG THE WAY

∞

I always wondered why my love of history and the value that I gave it throughout my life was so high. I concluded that from early life, my history affected me. There's no doubt the traumas I experienced at a young age were responsible for the trajectory I followed, even up until now.

I always loved history because of some of the teachers that influenced me throughout my education. My later years in primary school taught me the basics of Canadian and, to some extent, world history but it was in a skewed way as it left out very important participants in Canadian history – indigenous history. Later in life I would recognize that and it would help me enhance my knowledge in a more balanced way to include even the parts of our history that shame us and make us sad.

My high school education included history teachers that encouraged me to learn and made that learning more fun, but serious and real. I particularly remember my Grade 9 history teacher. She was very good at bringing royalty to life and making it more real for a young girl. I also appreciate my Grade 10 history teacher who treated me with respect despite some of my challenges at that time and teenage angst. He brought history to life and made it current.

My college and university professors and teaching assistants taught me history, but more importantly, how to think for myself and understand some of the "whys" that explained our history. That would become incredibly important to me as I tried to unravel the mystery of my post-traumatic stress.

I would go as far as saying that this pattern of my history and education saved my life more than once by helping me understand myself and why I reacted the way I did. Knowledge is strength and the more we know, even the unpleasant things, the better we can respond to them.

I wonder if my history teachers will ever know the impact they had on my life.

POWER OF THOUGHTS

∞

Another big learning for me was recognizing the power of choosing my thoughts. We acknowledge the importance of paying attention to what food we consume for our physical health, but rarely pay attention to monitor the thoughts we consume. This is a key shift as the thoughts we choose and the meaning we attach to those thoughts will determine our reality.

It's a worthwhile exercise to get more intentional about sifting through the inner dialogue that takes up space in our minds and deciding whether it serves us to allow it to take up space in our head. If we change our thoughts, we can change our outcomes.

According to the Cleveland Clinic, the average person has 60,000 thoughts per day, 95% of which repeat each day. Sadly, 80% of those repeated thoughts are negative on average. Consider how destructive that kind of negative repetition is on our well-being. Instead, what if we chose to flip the negative stories we tell ourselves and settle on more positive versions or meanings. Our brain believes what we tell it, so our expectations are often realized (the good, the bad, and the ugly). If we work at choosing more positive meanings to attach to our thoughts, we increase the chance for better realities.

Be sure that choosing this power of thought is hard work, especially when experiencing PTS symptoms. Choice isn't always immediately available if the panic and fear is strong. But paying attention to what we say to ourselves is very powerful and can really impact our inner peace and ability to live a good life. It's well worth the effort.

BE KIND TO YOURSELF

∞

Tied to managing our thoughts, I invite you to be kind to yourself. It took me a long time to be able to do this. As humans, we're not perfect. Forgive yourself your imperfections. Get comfortable in your own skin. Reconnect with yourself. Get grounded and centred in and with yourself. Avoid searching for your sense of self from external sources (i.e. what other people think or say about you) and instead, seek your sense of self internally.

SPIRITUALITY: BRUISED BUT NEVER BROKEN

∞

My spirituality was probably the most affected part of me because of my past experiences and assaults. This is because two of my attackers were also "men of the cloth" and supposed to strengthen my spiritual being. I can tell you assault is so far from that and really impacts spiritual growth and beliefs.

Fortunately, I also had a very strong base of spirituality every day in life with my family and most of their close friends and relatives. I recall this always adding to my belief that most people were good and honourable. There were only a few who did me wrong, and I could not hold the entire religious community responsible for their crimes.

It also made me believe that not all religious people were "good" people and could do horrible things. History also taught me this, as many things are perpetrated by human beings in the name of religion. I only had to look as far as Northern Ireland where horrible things were done to people based on their religion, even though in my mind, the "troubles" in Northern Ireland were more economic based and religion made it easier for those in power to justify their oppression and convince people to follow them.

I was raised in a Protestant church and recall some of the "hell fire" and god- fearing teachings of the church. In my young life, and in this, my mature life, I see God, the Creator, whatever our culture calls a higher power, as one of love, community, and most of all, Peace. My faith and spirituality should bring me peace; not fear. I should believe in a higher power because of the goodness, direction, and guidance that it brings to life, rather than a fear of the alternative.

That is where I am now. My spirituality tells me I am part of a bigger world, but I can play an important role in its existence and growth. I can influence myself and others to take care of a world that has seen so much pain and abuse in its history. I can question the validity of others without harming my own spirit. I can question why organized religion can ignore or avoid the most difficult questions we have of them; all in an effort to protect themselves.

I can question how trying to hide a painful history will somehow "make it go away" and only repeat itself. I can believe that dealing with our difficult pasts will break a cycle of violence, and help us move forward to a more peaceful, compassionate, and spiritual life with others.

My spirit was definitely bruised along the way, but because of the good influencers around me, it was not broken. I thank them for that gift.

FULL CIRCLE: THROUGH THE EYE OF A CHILD AT LAST

∞

Another of the recurring themes or patterns in my life was my creativity. Childhood allows us to be creative, to think independently and see our future life with awe and with no limits. I was no different as a child, and in some ways, this innocence is what saved me over and over again.

I was a creative child. I loved art, music, and writing. It always inspired me and provided an escape from the more mundane things we do every day. My mother was one of those mothers who kept some of the things I had created as a child. Fortunately, I also have something that she created as a child, a little piece of pottery with flowers painted on it that she had given her mother in 1942. Yes, her mother, my grandmother, must have loved it as she wrote on the bottom of it to remind her where it came from. I look back at it now and appreciate these memories that bring back a childhood of love and peace.

It is this creativity that I think saved me as mentioned before. I could escape into the wallpaper on the walls when things were not good. I remember a doctor telling me this was an escape for some children being abused to help them through the pain and hurt. I remember being floored when she told me this because I recalled doing this and the memory of some wallpapers in my room, and others, became very vivid in my mind as an adult.

I recently went to a museum where I live and was really impacted by what I saw. One item in particular really brought me full circle. It was a miniature sculpture of a bird sitting on top of its cage, and a girl inside the cage sitting on a perch. I felt like that girl many times growing up. The wonderful part of that sculpture was the wonderful memory that it brought back. My aunt and uncle always had a budgie. I remember the budgie flying around, sitting on my shoulder, helping me eat my breakfast and talking to us.

The creativity that I saw told me that I could see life through the eyes of a child, rather than having to recall the "adult" situations I had been put in way too young, and the violence I experienced as a child. It took such a long time to see life with that creativity and innocence again.

MAKING SOME SENSE OF IT ALL

∞

As you can well imagine, the confusion and chaos of post-traumatic stress can have a huge impact on the person suffering and recovering, as well as those around them. One of the things that hit me hardest was the impact it had on my family as they, too, never chose that life. It was forced upon them as much as it was me. They, too had to deal with the biases, the judgement, and the stereotypes that were forced on victims of crime. It forced them to learn about and deal with things that human beings shouldn't have to face.

In my case, and in many others, it's complicated even more when it's thrust upon us at an early age when our brain and our mind has not yet developed and we're experiencing emotions and pain that no child should ever know. Sexual assault is not about sex. It's about violence. It's about loss of control over one's own body and soul. It's about humiliation.

My family was one of service to others, including policing and public safety, and the military. I was brought up in that environment and it impacted me. All of this made me realize at a very young age that the world wasn't always a safe place. That being said, I grew up as an optimist, always seeing the good in people until they proved otherwise. I knew about service to others at a very young age, along with the sacrifice that goes along with that. Christmas was different for my family as my father sometimes had to work different shifts. Yet we celebrated it and loved our shared time together.

The confusion and chaos of unprocessed memories, of my own experiences and those of people close to me, were relentless for a number of years until I was able to get professional help to sort it out and manage the symptoms of post-traumatic stress. It took years to do that. Post-traumatic stress has been overcome in my life but I will always have to manage it so it doesn't recur with a vengeance again.

The accumulation of the stress from the memories caused me to experience severe and often psychologically violent symptoms. I've often heard people say that the military and police officers who suffer from PTSD knew it was a risk and signed up for it anyway. That's not true. Nobody signs up for this. We've only come to understand it recently. I don't think we realize the huge impacts of our own experience and memories until we experience the affects personally. It's horrendous.

It also made me realize that my own experience was an important, but small part of my post-traumatic stress symptoms. I often felt that I was only one person in a much bigger world, and my experiences were inconsequential in the big scheme of things. I felt that nobody cared about my experiences as they were more concerned with their own issues. It made me realize that my PTSD symptoms were only part of who I was and am. They no longer define me. The world around me scared me more. I felt like a grain of sand in a vast world. It took years to recognize even that grain of sand is an important part of the whole picture.

We can overcome it. I can't stress enough how important it is to ask for professional help when we recognize the increased anxiety we experience. Asking for help is not a weakness, it's a huge strength. I used to consider myself weak for experiencing symptoms of PTS but now realize that it's a great strength to be able to survive my past and share it with others to increase awareness of the mental health challenges we face after repeated psychological traumas.

It's given me a unique, though not solitary, perspective, where I was able to analyze the story as someone with lived experience as a victim, a survivor, and related professional expertise. Importantly, it also comes at a time where we recognize that the past can't be changed, but it must be acknowledged. We can move forward with those impacted by a very unkind past and change the way we do things in the future.

We often choose the easiest way to do things but the easiest is not often the best way. Change is difficult and sometimes painful. Only an accumulation of diverse thought, perspective, and solutions will allow us to move past the hurt of our history. That's why I am here to add my introspective input to a very complicated past and try to contribute to a better future.

The world has finally been kind to me. Our current history, and recent events in Canadian history, have proven to me that I am not alone. Yet I hope I am able to help with some of the hard work required to move forward in a positive way and acknowledge the tremendous contribution given to us by those affected by psychological trauma. We are just now allowing ourselves to admit and acknowledge the amount of psychological trauma that many have survived. Much of what we learn comes from experience and their contribution to recovery is immeasurable. That experience is difficult to explain to somebody who hasn't experienced it first-hand. Nobody should have to do this hard work alone.

I hope this book has given people a better understanding of the symptoms of post-traumatic stress and recognize that we are all connected and everything can impact our psyche. Tread lightly as you support those affected and let them lead their own healing. People often feel that they know best, but they don't always. We have unique ways of narrating our own stories and they're all valid.

My words have finally been heard. I hope they can help at least one person.

ENHANCE YOUR EXPERIENCE AND UNDERSTANDING OF THIS BOOK

Books that helped me heal!

The books that I read during my college years by Viktor E. Frankl and R.D. Laing came back to me in surprising detail many years later. In retrospect, that was during a time when I was trying to understand what was happening in my mind.

Viktor E. Frankl – Man's Search for Meaning (Beacon Press, Boston, Massachusetts; ©1959, 1962, 1984, 1992, 2006, 2014 by Viktor E. Frankl)

R.D. Laing – The Politics of the Family (Random House Inc, January 1, 1972)

This book by Martha Stout was recommended to me by my psychologist after I had been receiving treatment for my symptoms for a while. It helped me understand what I was going through as well as what I was not going through. This book contained many words of wisdom that I was able to apply to my life during my recovery. One that stands out the most is:

"The true remedies are making a safe place, finding out, remembering, not hiding from the memories, and not blaming."

Martha Stout – The Myth of Sanity; (Penguin Books, Feb. 26, 2002)

Historical Novels that gave me perspective and helped me understand my own circumstance better:

James Bartleman – As Long as the Rivers Flow, A Novel (Alfred A. Knopf, A Division of Random House of Canada Limited, Canada, 2011; ©2011 James Bartleman)

John Grisham – A Time to Kill (March 15, 2004 by Dell)

Leon Uris – Trinity (Doubleday, 1976)

Leon Uris – Redemption (HarperCollins, 1995)

Jill and Leon Uris – A Terrible Beauty (March 1, 1982 by Bantam Books)

I have the honour of calling Cindy Watson my coach and mentor. She has seen me through much of the writing, all of the editing and publication of this book. Her calm demeanour, wealth of knowledge, compassion and understanding has grounded me and allowed me to tell my story with dignity, some grace, and much love and understanding in an effort to increase the awareness of mental health challenges in today's world.

Cindy Watson – The Art of Feminine Negotiation (Morgan James, 2023, ©2023 Cindy Watson)

Songs that helped me heal!

Blue Rodeo – Try (Risque Disque under Licence to WEA Music of Canada, Ltd.; 1986, 1987)

Barclay James Harvest – A Child of the Universe (Polydor, June, 1974)

ACKNOWLEDGEMENTS

My first acknowledgement goes to my long-time Psychologist, Judi Hashmall, Med.,C.Psych.Associate, who provided her compassion, understanding, amazing listening skills, and utmost professionalism during a time when I needed her most. I credit her with keeping me alive to eventually be able to live a productive life again and focus on my passions.

My second acknowledgement goes to my coach and mentor, Cindy Watson, Founder of Women On Purpose who provided her compassion, understanding, amazing listening skills, and utmost professionalism during a time when I needed her most. Yes, there's a pattern here! I credit Cindy with guiding; not directing, as I wrote and grappled with the content of this book. She ensured this story was mine to tell, but she helped me with clarity during the difficult and repetitive moments. Yes, PTS symptoms does include some jumbled thoughts and repetitive words.

Thirdly, I'd like to acknowledge my Counsellor, John Taylor, MSW, RSW, who provides compassion, understanding, and utmost professionalism to keep me sane. He ensures that I continue to look after my mental health and appreciate the woman I have become.

I'd like to acknowledge my sister, Kathryn and friends, who reviewed this manuscript and provided valuable feedback.

Words can't describe the love and support I've received from my immediate family during my entire lifetime. My journey through life has also impacted them and made their lives more difficult at times. They've been with me throughout and I've never doubted their love and support.

My extended family fills me with mixed feelings. For the most part, they have been amazing. At times, several have added to the symptoms that made life difficult. Several, including a few aunts and uncles have provided so much love and support and I can't thank them enough. They've had such a wonderful impact on me over the years, and I also credit them with keeping me alive.

My friends who have walked with me during this journey have been wonderful. Sometimes their words have provided comfort and understanding. Sometimes just being there has been the strength that was needed at that time. Words can't thank you enough.

My history teachers, teaching assistants, college and university professors have given me the ability to think, analyse and understand events around me. Thank you for that!

My first counsellor during my teenage years, Gord, gave me the understanding to forgive myself and not blame myself for events that happened in my younger years. He gave me self confidence to know that my life was valuable and I was worthy of love and compassion. He also helped me make better choices moving forward. Thank you!

ABOUT THE AUTHOR

Peggy was born in Toronto in September, 1956. She lived most of her life in that city with a few exceptions in her young years and an 18-year period when she lived about an hour and a half north of the city.

She graduated from the University of Toronto in 1981 with a Bachelor of Arts degree, focusing on History, Celtic Studies, Criminology, Political Science and Philosophy. Those subjects had a huge impact on her personal life then and over the years.

Peggy went on to work in Financial Services, both branch banking and later Technology & Operations. She took an early retirement in 2002 to recover from health issues and moved north 2 years later. She was able to find meaning by volunteering with the local police department and eventually found full time employment in public safety.

Peggy retired in 2021 and moved back to her hometown, Toronto closer to her family again. During this time, and for years before, she has provided support and personal experience to initiatives to raise awareness of mental health challenges. That is her passion because no human being should have to face the challenges that she faced in her personal life's journey without love and support.

This book is a labour of that passion, commitment and love.